THE TEEN'S ULTIMATE GUIDE TO

Making Money When You Can't Get a Job

199 IDEAS FOR EARNING CASH ON YOUR OWN TERMS

By Julie Fryer

The Teen's Ultimate Guide to Making Money When You Can't Get a Job: 199 Ideas for Earning Cash On Your Own Terms

Copyright © 2012 by Atlantic Publishing Group, Inc.
1210 SW 23rd Place • Ocala, Florida 34471 • Ph: 800-814-1132 • Fax: 352-622-1875
Website: www.atlantic-pub.com • Email: sales@atlantic-pub.com
SAN Number: 268-1250

Library of Congress Cataloging-in-Publication Data

Fryer, Julie.
  The teen's ultimate guide to making money when you can't get a job : 199 ideas for earning cash on your own terms / Julie Fryer.
     p. cm.
  Includes bibliographical references and index.
  ISBN 978-1-60138-611-3 (alk. paper) -- ISBN 1-60138-611-7 1. Money making projects for children--Juvenile literature. 2. Teenagers--Employment--Juvenile literature. 3. Small business--Juvenile literature. 4. Young businesspeople--Juvenile literature. I. Title.
  HF5392.F79 2012
  650.1'20835--dc23
                          2012015628

Printed in the United States
PROJECT MANAGER: Gretchen Pressley
BOOK PRODUCTION DESIGN: T.L. Price • design@tlpricefreelance.com
PROOFREADING: C&P Marse • bluemoon6749@bellsouth.net
COVER DESIGNS: Jackie Miller • millerjackiej@gmail.com

Printed on Recycled Paper

A few years back we lost our beloved pet dog Bear, who was not only our best and dearest friend but also the "Vice President of Sunshine" here at Atlantic Publishing. He did not receive a salary but worked tirelessly 24 hours a day to please his parents.

Bear was a rescue dog who turned around and showered myself, my wife, Sherri, his grandparents Jean, Bob, and Nancy, and every person and animal he met (well, maybe not rabbits) with friendship and love. He made a lot of people smile every day.

We wanted you to know a portion of the profits of this book will be donated in Bear's memory to local animal shelters, parks, conservation organizations, and other individuals and nonprofit organizations in need of assistance.

– Douglas & Sherri Brown

PS: We have since adopted two more rescue dogs: first Scout, and the following year, Ginger. They were both mixed golden retrievers who needed a home.

Want to help animals and the world? Here are a dozen easy suggestions you and your family can implement today:

- *Adopt and rescue a pet from a local shelter.*
- *Support local and no-kill animal shelters.*
- *Plant a tree to honor someone you love.*
- *Be a developer — put up some birdhouses.*
- *Buy live, potted Christmas trees and replant them.*
- *Make sure you spend time with your animals each day.*
- *Save natural resources by recycling and buying recycled products.*
- *Drink tap water, or filter your own water at home.*
- *Whenever possible, limit your use of or do not use pesticides.*
- *If you eat seafood, make sustainable choices.*
- *Support your local farmers market.*
- *Get outside. Visit a park, volunteer, walk your dog, or ride your bike.*

Five years ago, Atlantic Publishing signed the Green Press Initiative. These guidelines promote environmentally friendly practices, such as using recycled stock and vegetable-based inks, avoiding waste, choosing energy-efficient resources, and promoting a no-pulping policy. We now use 100-percent recycled stock on all our books. The results: in one year, switching to post-consumer recycled stock saved 24 mature trees, 5,000 gallons of water, the equivalent of the total energy used for one home in a year, and the equivalent of the greenhouse gases from one car driven for a year.

Author dedication

This book is dedicated to my devoted family: my husband, Pete for putting up with me when I'm on deadline; my oldest son, Sam, for letting me use his story in the book; and our youngest, Nick, for always keeping life interesting. Thanks, guys. I love you!

I would also like to thank all the amazing young people I met while writing this book. What an honor to hear your inspiring stories! I truly appreciate all your help.

Table of Contents

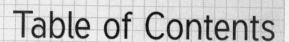

Chapter 2: Finding Ways to Make Money

Chapter 3: Computer and Tech-Savvy Jobs

Chapter 4: Make Money with Your Hobbies and Interests

Chapter 5: Make Money Doing the Dirty Work 133

Chapter 6: Make Money by Helping Out 163

Chapter 7: Make Money by Selling Things 213

Chapter 8: A Few Business Basics.......237

Chapter 9: A Few Money Basics...........259

Chapter 10: Beyond the Basics 285

Chapter 11: Your Business Future 303

You Can Do It!.................313

Appendix A: Sample Business Documents 315

Introduction

There's one constant when it comes to being a teenager — you need money. You know it, your parents know it, and you've probably spread the word to all willing relatives as holidays and birthdays approach. Next to birthdays and "the Bank of Mom and Dad," though, the only sure way to get money is to earn it. The question is: How in this economy are you going to find a way to put money in your pocket? If you've been out looking for jobs, you know how few jobs are available, even if you're looking for just a few hours

a week. If you have not started filling out applications, here's a sobering statistic: As of October 2011, the national unemployment rate for youth ages 16 to 19 was 24.1 percent. Sadly, this is an improvement from 2010, when the youth unemployment rate hit a record high of more than 27 percent. These statistics do not count those under 16 looking for work or teens who have just plain given up. For the most up-to-date statistics, visit the Bureau of Labor Statistics website at **www.bls.gov**.

This situation mirrors the overall national unemployment rate that for the years 2010 and 2011 averaged at above 9 percent. These are jobless levels not seen since the early 1980s. It's the highest unemployment rate recorded in your lifetime, and probably in your parents' lifetimes, according to the Bureau of Labor Statistics. Complicating matters further, the average length of unemployment is 40.6 weeks, which means a high percentage of people have been out of work for three-fourths of a year. These once well-employed people are forced to take part-time, minimum wage jobs to make ends meet and keep the bills paid. Not so long ago, these part-time jobs were filled by teens. Now when you go apply for a job, you're competing against older, more experienced workers desperate for any kind of employment.

Another consequence of this struggling economy is an overall downturn in business, which translates into employers hiring fewer workers and cutting back hours of existing staff. So, there's more competition for the jobs out there, and even if you find a job, you might not get many hours. The direst news of all, though, is there seems to be no end in sight for the economic downturn. Many analysts consider this a tipping point and think employment levels might never return to previous highs. As a young worker, this can be depressing. So, what's a teen to do for money?

How This Book Can Help

For starters, don't be discouraged. You've taken an important step in picking up this book. This guide will turn these scary statistics around and give you step-by-step directions for finding what you like to do, offer brainstorming ideas for making money on your own, and provide information on how to find people to pay you. Just because jobs are scarce — and getting scarcer — does not mean you can't find plenty of ways to make money. People are willing to pay for things they don't want to do themselves. Teens always have taken these odd jobs such as babysitting or lawn mowing, and they are still acceptable ways to make money. This book, however, will help you go beyond the obvious job ideas, so you can enjoy making money and fit work into your hectic schedule. It will show you that you don't need a "regular job" to survive. And it will show you how to elevate your passion and make money doing the things you love.

VOCAB

This book considers a **regular job** to be a job in which you work for someone else, you punch a clock, or you don't have control over when, how, or where you work. An example would be working part time at a fast-food chain.

If you've already peeked ahead through the job ideas, you've seen that this book has nearly 200 ideas for making money on your own, and that's just the beginning. The chapters divide up the general skill sets but overlap in many ways and can be combined to best meet your unique skills and interests. Any one of these ideas is ready to go, but they are also a great place to start brainstorming. Once you've explored the options here, you might realize that working for yourself will be better than a regular job both for your finances and your busy life.

In addition to great job ideas, this book will walk you through the process of working for yourself and include concrete information on developing your ideas, getting things started, and finding customers. It will also include a beginner's guide to banking, investing, and taxes; job performance tips and marketing ideas; thoughts on taking jobs with you to college; and all the other nitty-gritty details you need to succeed. Throughout the book will be stories of teens who have been able to make money on their own terms. There is, of course, the potential for loss or mistakes when going out on your own, and later chapters will address these issues. Before you start ordering equipment or business cards, it's a good idea at least to skim through the entire book.

How I Know What I'm Talking About

Before we continue too far, I would like to share a bit about my life and the personal experience I have with this topic. I've been self-employed as a freelance writer since 1997. I have dealt with every issue you will have to face, including finding customers, scheduling my workday, handling payment and non-payment, dealing with clients, and developing my business. It's not easy to work for myself, but overall, I love it. To be fair, I did have a ten-year writing career and college degree behind me when I went out on my own — and this experience did make it easier to find work. I've found, though, that young people have fresh outlooks and can add some energy to any project. In my opinion, the good definitely outweighs the bad, and I can't imagine holding down a regular job.

I decided to take on writing this particular subject because I not only know a lot about self-employment, but I'm also the mom of teenager who needs money but does not have much free time. My son, Sam, is 16 and is, for all accounts, a typical teenager. He's a junior and is taking as many AP classes as possible. He is involved in varsity sports; is active in FFA and other local service clubs; loves to hunt, fish, and play video games; cannot miss the ESPN nightly report; religiously follows his fantasy football team, the Minnesota Vikings, and Minnesota Twins; drives a beat-up old car that guzzles gas; works school concessions to earn money for next year's senior trip; is planning a summer canoe trip; is trying to save money for prom, college, and more hunting gear; and can't really commit to a regular job. Sound familiar? I'm sure you have the same busy, hectic schedule.

Just because you have no time for a job doesn't mean you do not need money — and our backyard money tree is not producing very well. So, over the last two years, Sam (with my help) has found ways to make money for himself. We live in a rural area, so he's been able to find work for farmers and has done everything from haying to digging tiling trenches. He's also taken on babysitting jobs for me and yard work jobs for our friends and neighbors. He's helped me sort through all my garage sale finds and started listing things to sell online. His path really has been the definition of odd jobs, but it has worked out well with his busy schedule and has given him money to spend and save.

Through these experiences, Sam has learned a bit about dealing with customers, putting in a hard day's work, and doing the legwork to find new jobs. He's learned the value of referrals and word-of-mouth and even picked up a few new skills along the way. We got him a bank account, so he can manage his money, and we joined a stock market website to grow his money a bit before college rolls around. It's definitely been an interesting time for both of us, and we have each learned a lot. I am excited to write this book and am looking forward to sharing our ideas and research with you. I'm also keeping Sam on retainer to review the book and warn me if I start acting too much like a "mom."

How to Keep Your Priorities Straight

Finally, one last message before you begin your work journey — and I'm sure your parents would agree with me. Your No. 1 job right now is to succeed at high school. Good grades, well-rounded extracurricular activities, and time with your friends and family are the most important aspects of your life. Doing well in school and enjoying the last of your teen years will give you a good base for the rest of your life. Sure, money is important and has to be addressed. However, as a teen, making money should be way down at the bottom of your priority list. Once you add work to your schedule, it's easy to let things slip or tip out of balance, and it's very hard to get your GPA back once it starts to slide. You have many years of work ahead of you, but you will only have these high school and college years once in your life. Enjoy them, and don't stress too much about making money.

CHAPTER ONE

What is Self-Employment and Why Should You Consider It?

What does working for yourself really mean? At the most basic level, it means you aren't working for anyone — no one else profits or benefits from your labor. When you have a regular job, your employer benefits from your work. Consider this example: You get hired by Bud's Lawn Service to mow lawns this summer, and he pays you $8 per hour. Bud finds the customers, buys the equipment, arranges your schedule, and handles the billings — and charges his customers $20 per hour. He collects $12 per hour from your work to pay his business expenses and make a profit. All you have to do is show up, do your job, and collect your paycheck.

When you work for yourself, you have to do everything Bud does, but you also get to keep all the money leftover after you meet your expenses. In this case, working for Bud gives you a sure way to make money, but you'll make a lower amount. Working for yourself means you'll have to handle all the details, have a little less guarantee of a paycheck, but probably will make more money in the end. Either route to making money is acceptable — you just need to decide how much time and effort you're willing to put in and whether the rewards outweigh the risks.

A regular job — if you can find it — is definitely the surest route to making money. To work a regular job, though, you'll be giving up your time, freedom, and flexibility. You most likely will be doing monotonous tasks, have to be there at a certain time, and be under the direction of other people. Some of the tasks you'll take on as a self-employed worker also can be boring, but you at least will be trading your time on your own terms. The last four chapters of this book will cover the details needed to make your decision; for now let's talk about the options available to the self-employed.

From Babysitter to CEO

From teachers who substitute in your school to your favorite "free agent" football player, the self-employed work in every segment and for every company. Even big-name Fortune 500 companies hire self-employed consultants to step in temporarily when their corporations hit times of trouble. Often called subcontractors or independents, these people fill in when needed and don't collect benefits. Instead of becoming a standard employee, the consultant does a specific job and handles all the administrative, tax, and legal issues on his or her own. Many times the work they do — such as computer repair — is done through a written contract with specific guidelines, deadlines, and dollar amounts. Hiring subcontractors allows businesses to fill in staff during especially busy times without taking on the additional costs and hassles of keeping a permanent employee. It also gives businesses a way to find workers on a project-by-project basis so they can hire the best talent suited for each project's needs.

Self-employment also covers those running their own businesses. They can be any size, from a one-person operation to a multinational corporation. If you are the owner and operator of a business, you are self-employed. Independents work in any field available to the regular workforce, from catering to lawn care to interior design to computer programming. Some have come into self-employment out of necessity because they can't find a job elsewhere. Others choose to work for themselves because they don't want to deal with commitment or the hassles of working for someone else. Generally, these people do their work on an as-needed basis and sometimes contract with others for the long term. The spectrum is wide, but it has one common denominator: Self-employed people are in charge of their work life. Success or failure depends completely on your individual decisions, work ethic, and motivation.

Self-employment goes by many names, which are used as a way to assign you a title in the world of work so people know where you fit in. It doesn't matter what you call yourself as long as you're making money. When you are looking in some specific industries, however, you'll need to look for these broad terms used in that industry. These include:

- Freelancer. This term is used in the advertising, marketing, graphic design, and writing fields.

- Subcontractor or independent contractor. This is someone paid a prearranged fee to complete a specific job. A contract is drawn up outlining the project.

- Sole proprietorship. This refers to a business with one person owning and managing every aspect of the business.

- Consultant. As the name implies, this worker provides consultation in a specific area such as finance or computer programming.
- Apprentice. Used for beginners in technical fields such as in plumbing or electrical work
- Assistant or aide. Someone who assists another in a specific job such as a secretary. This is sometimes called "virtual assistant" when work is done online or remotely.
- Transcriptionist or translator. Someone who enters data from written or typed documents or translates writing from one language to another

---

VOCAB

In your search for self-employment, you'll hear the term **entrepreneur** used frequently. This term has become synonymous with someone who has gone out on his or her own, found a unique business idea, or done very well in a short amount of time. You'll hear stories of young entrepreneurs who have hit the big time with small, simple ideas. These ideas often grow into huge, national enterprises that reap large sums of money, prestige, and success. People most often view an entrepreneur as someone who takes on higher risk to establish his or her business. It's also a term that is frequently overused to describe just about any type of business owner. Call yourself an entrepreneur if you'd like, but it doesn't matter if you're an entrepreneur or a lawn boy. As long as you're managing your own moneymaking, you are self-employed.

What Does It Take to Work for Yourself?

Going out on your own does require a broader skill set than holding down a regular job. You are the boss, which means you and you alone are responsible for every aspect of the operation. You'll have to handle everything from finding customers to doing the labor to collecting payment. You'll have to do tasks that might not be interesting to you and, in fact, might be chores you will have to learn how to do. Some of these tasks also fall squarely into the "non-billable" hours category, which means you'll have to put time into work you are not paid for. An example would be starting up a cookie-baking business — you might love baking cookies, but you'll also have to handle packaging, transportation, permit applications, and customer service. Acquiring these skills can be beneficial but might not be the most exciting part of your job. Honestly, though, it still probably beats flipping burgers for four hours a day.

VOCAB

Non-billable hours are hours worked that cannot be billed to the customer, such as time spent maintaining your equipment. **Billable hours** are those that can be charged to the client, such as the actual time spent mowing the lawn.

To decide if self-employment is for you, it's best to start by weighing the pros and cons. Ironically, some the advantages are also some of the disadvantages, and it really depends on your personality and work style if you can handle the rigors of working for yourself. You will have no clocks to punch and no bosses to answer to. It also means there are *no* clocks to punch and *no* bosses to answer to. Without self-motivation, you will not succeed as an independent worker. You must be a self-starter because without a set schedule or someone to answer to, you are the only one who can "make" you work. The pros and cons also depend on the type of jobs you decide to do and are helpful to consider as you start formulating your ideas.

Advantages

In this economy, one of the biggest advantages of working for yourself is just that. You do not have to rely on others for employment or adequate wages. You control your own destiny — and can make as much money as you're willing to work for. Compared to regular teen jobs such as those at fast-food chains, you'll also acquire a wide-ranging set of skills that translate well to college and beyond. Other general advantages you'll gain when you are the boss:

- Flexibility. You'll be able to set your own schedule to work around your studies and extra activities. You can take the days off you want — if you do not want to work holidays or weekend nights, you do not have to.

- Interest. You can pursue jobs that match your interests instead of putting in time at an entry-level job.

- Finances. Once things are up and running, you most likely will make more than the minimum wages offered at most part-time jobs.

- Skill development. If you choose a field you are interested in, your work time also becomes time spent honing those skills. As your skills improve, you can add more to your offerings and potentially increase your prices. You'll also develop additional skills needed to run your business.

- Mentor building. You can work alongside more experienced mentors and learn from them as you go. Search out people who are good at what they do and become their assistant.

- Reference and résumé building. A successful venture looks great on a college application, and you can build a strong collection of references from your customers. Keep a journal of your work history, and document everything including positive comments or problems you solved.

- Potential. You can build an operation that could go with you to college or potentially grow into a full-fledged business.

- Pride and success. Knowing you have done something this big on your own is a great self-esteem boost and a great step toward adulthood.

TIP!

Most experts recommend that teens work no more than 20 hours per week during the school year. Avoid working late hours that will shortchange your sleep, and do not work for more than four hours per day during the week or eight hours per day on weekends.

Disadvantages

Working in any job is a great way to build skills you will need for the rest of your working life. A job will teach you how to follow detailed instructions, keep a schedule and arrive on time, deal with people and solve problems, and fit into a working environment. A regular job also gives you the added bonus of learning from a more experienced mentor. The lack of mentors and this directed learning are the biggest disadvantages of working for yourself. Seeking out mentors or asking your parents to guide you can alleviate this. *Chapter 11 will cover finding and working with mentors.*

As mentioned previously, many of the disadvantages also can be advantages to helping you learn, grow, and become a better businessperson. It's important, though, to understand what you're signing up for before you jump into self-employment. Some of these two-sided drawbacks include:

- Establishing a work history. Listing self-employed on a résumé is often a red flag for employers because they have no way of checking your previous work. Be sure to ask for references from every customer, keep a detailed journal of the work you do, and keep these handy for résumés and future references.

- Motivation. Without a set schedule and required hours, it's easy to procrastinate and put the work off. You must be a self-starter, be willing to plan ahead, and be motivated to stick to your plan.

- Finances. You might make more money, but you will not have a regular payday and will have to collect from your customers — some of whom might avoid paying. You'll also have to be more disciplined with your money and bank a little away to cover dry spells between paying customers.

- Non-interesting activities. You might have to step out of your comfort zone to achieve your goal. For example, you might love making funky earrings, but to sell them, you might have to make some cold calls or deal with the public face-to-face. These will be character-building activities — if you're willing to do the non-fun stuff to achieve your dream.

- Taxes. With a regular job, the employer collects taxes before you get your paycheck. Self-employed people must record, file, and submit payroll taxes on their own. *Taxes and legal issues will be covered in Chapter 10.*

- Legal issues. As with taxes, any legalities related to your chosen job, such as permits, are your responsibility to understand and acquire. You also take on all the risks if something goes wrong, such as loss of data when working with a computer.

- Time commitment. As mentioned earlier, you'll have non-billable hours that can take time to manage. In addition, when you really enjoy what you are doing, you might put too much time into the effort. This would be great for business, but not so good for those priorities we talked about earlier.

- Stress. Working for yourself can be more stressful than a regular job because you know everything is riding on your shoulders, and if you fail, you don't make any money.

CASE STUDY: ON THE JOB WITH BARRY WEINSTEIN

Occupation: Product development
and CEO Pillowcase Studies
Age: Started his business at age 19
pillowcasestudies@gmail.com
www.pillowcasestudies.com

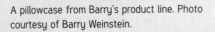

A pillowcase from Barry's product line. Photo courtesy of Barry Weinstein.

I've had an entrepreneurial spirit since I was a kid, and I started my first moneymaking project back in fourth grade selling wristbands to my classmates. Over the years, I tried a few more ideas and made some decent money, especially compared to other kids my age. My big idea came when I was a sophomore in college. I came up with the idea after falling asleep on my textbook and realizing that it would be nice if the textbook were fluffier. This was the beginning of Pillowcase Studies, my company specializing in creatively designed, academically oriented printed pillowcases.

Developing my good idea into a real product, though, was challenging, and it took a few stops-and-starts before I assembled a great team of graphic artists, Web designers, and a high-quality printer. Believe it or not, I found most of my team through a posting on Craigslist. Even with this amazing team, I needed to invest money and time up front before we could put everything in place to actually print the pillowcases and bring them to market. Which means it took a while before I started seeing a return on investment, and when I did make money, I put it right back into my company.

After the prototypes and initial batches came out, I started getting offers from investors, which I declined. I've always been confident in this product, and I wanted to let the market decide if it was effective. I've handled most of the administrative duties, such as sourcing the product, setting up all my business accounts, dealing with taxes, and spearheading the marketing campaign. I also learned to ignore the naysayers — I knew a good product with good marketing would sell.

I started my marketing by going on Facebook™ — in other words, free advertising — and telling all 1,100 of my "friends" about the product and sending them a link to our website. Soon feedback and word-of-mouth took over — also free — and I was getting orders from people I didn't even know. I think this approach has worked for us because we have such a unique product, and once one person sees the product, the buzz quickly spreads through the campuses. Business continues to grow and I'm planning to stick with this after college.

Words of Wisdom: Learn everything you can from every job you take. Even mistakes are learning opportunities. Even if you lose money on an idea, you will gain an experience to take with you.

Unique opportunities

Even with the many disadvantages, working for yourself will give you access to opportunities you would not have otherwise. Sure, you'll have to handle problems outside your comfort zone, but in the end, you'll gain skills transferable to your future college studies and professional career. You'll be exposed to situations and people you could never find at a regular job. You also have the great possibility of meeting a mentor or expert who can help you along and guide you down the right path. Finally, you'll be able to try lots of new things without the big commitment of a job — if you find that you don't like what you're doing, you don't have to continue. You can easily stop, revise your plan, and head off in a new direction.

So, what do you think so far? Is working for yourself sounding like a good option? Do you think you can handle the rigors, or would you be happier punching a clock? Either answer is right as long as you're happy with it. Any type of work really boils down to deciding what you're willing to trade your time for. For example: To earn enough to go out to eat this weekend, you'll have to spend about two hours of your day working at the local fast food joint. Is this two hours of your time worth trading for that meal out? If the answer is yes, then you're ready to work. If it's not, then don't take a job, but you won't be able to go out to eat this weekend. If the answer is: "I want to make more than minimum wage and still be able to go out with my friends," then you're probably ready to be self-employed. Now you just need to determine how you are going to go about reaching that goal. Keep reading … you have lots more to learn.

CHAPTER TWO

Finding Ways to Make Money

Deciding how you are going to create your own job begins with a look at the kinds of work you have to choose from and an assessment of your interests and skills. A great starting point is to review the career assessment you took back in middle school. Do you remember that long list of questions you went through and the career choices results sheet you got back? Most schools give this assessment in seventh or eighth grade to help students define their interests and start considering possible career choices. These possibilities then help you plan your high school schedule, so you take the courses most applicable to future college planning.

Sometimes called aptitude tests, personality assessments, or interest inventories, the premise of the interest survey is to look at your personality and interests and then match you with career clusters where these traits are a good fit. There's no right or wrong answer, and these inventories are meant only to give you a good starting point for further exploration. Your parents probably have this filed away, or your school guidance counselor could give you a copy. That copy is a great tool to review now and use as a jumping-off point to come up with job ideas. You can also find numerous online inventories that give you instant results. Many of these online tools do charge a fee, which is not necessary unless you are heading off to college.

An easy-to-use and free interest inventory can be found at Learn More Indiana (**www.learnmoreindiana.org** — look for "career clickers"). You can complete these questions in less than five minutes and get a detailed list of your personal work style and possible careers that would fit you well. With this list, you can narrow down general career fields that will work well for you.

Do What You Love

You've probably learned at school that you do best in the subjects that most interest you. It's easy to study and pay attention to something when the topic keeps you thinking and awake. This same philosophy goes for your working life. If you enjoy your work and are doing something that fits your interests, you might look forward to going to work. Doing something you love isn't generally possible for most teen-level jobs. Most teens just "do their time," so they can earn money. When you choose self-employment, you have the luxury of creating a job you will, at least, somewhat enjoy and possibly even love. If you can make money with your idea, reach your financial goals, and still enjoy your working time, you're ahead of most of your peers.

TIP!

Be careful when turning your favorite pastime into your job. Even if you love something, you might lose interest if you're forced to do that activity for work.

To find your true loves, begin with writing up a list of your interests, skills, and hobbies. Start out general, and then narrow it down even further. Be open-minded and creative, and don't think about how much you can earn — right now, everything is possible. Review your school career assessment, and think about how these results relate to your personal interests list. Thinking about the three main jobs categories, can you find a pattern or an area where most of your hobbies fit? This is where you should start looking for work — and don't limit yourself to what you think people want or where you think you can earn the most money. You might have that unique combination of skills and interests people don't even know they need yet.

Do What You Like

The next step in honing your job plan is to look honestly at what you're willing to do for money. You might love playing with children, but are you willing or able to handle a dirty diaper? Using your list of ideas, examine what is required to accomplish that job. Do some basic online research by looking at professional sites that offer the same services or search for "how to" perform your job idea. Check your local library for information on the area you're thinking of working in. These results will show you the scope of services to consider and help you start to refine your idea. The search will also help you consider the unpleasant aspects of your job. Remember that comfort zone talked about earlier — are you willing to do every part of the job, even if it means doing something you do not like to do? Of course, every job includes challenging or uninteresting tasks, and sometimes you have to be willing to accept these tasks because you know the overall enjoyment you will get from the job is worth it.

Try the job out on your family and friends to see if they like it. You might find that your dream job has aspects to it you can't see yourself doing. That doesn't necessarily mean, though, that you have to dismiss that entire category of work. Using the dirty diaper example again: Just because you decide you can't handle diapers doesn't mean you can't still take on child-care jobs. You could just limit your babysitting service to kids that are potty-trained or older.

> ### TIP!
>
> Don't be afraid to try out a bunch of ideas. If you don't like the job after a few tries, you don't have to take on that work anymore. Just be careful not to commit too much money or time until you're sure you want to take something on.

When looking over your ideas, it's important to consider how that job will fit into your schedule. Tailor your job around the times of year that you have the most free time. A great what-not-to-do example of this would be the guy who decides to start a leaf-raking business. He's also a football player and soon finds that his favorite sport interferes with the one and only season when leaves need to be raked. To make money at raking leaves, he has to work in the fall, but that time of year is filled with practice, games, and a sore body on Saturday morning. However, if he wants to work in the lawn-care sector, he could find other yard chores that don't coincide with football — and hand off (no pun intended) the leaf-raking aspect of the business to a friend or sibling.

Consider the costs and risks

Next to what you're willing and able to do, you also need to look at the costs and risks associated with your particular choice. If you're thinking about work that requires special equipment or a license, can you afford to pay for that now before you start collecting money? Where will you store your equipment, or how will you haul it back and forth? *Chapter 8 will help you determine the costs of starting up and running a small business.* It's a good idea to keep these costs in mind as you review your plan.

Many jobs also pose unique safety issues. If your job requires using equipment such as a chain saw or hot stove, there's potential for injury. If you're handling other people's computers or technology, you risk losing data or damaging expensive components. If you're working with children, pets, or the elderly, you'll have their well-being in your hands. Many times, you'll be handed the keys to someone's home or given access to personal, confidential information. You'll be expected to protect these assets. *Job listings in chapters 3 through 7 will point out the potential risks with each individual job.* For now, though, keep in mind that when you work for yourself, you're taking all of the responsibility if something goes wrong. Thinking about these risks ahead of time will help you prepare and avoid making mistakes that lead to problems.

Also, be sure you know enough to do the job accurately, safely, and on time. This is not the place to bluff about your skills or abilities — too much can go wrong if you're unsure of what you're doing. However, no one expects a teen to be an expert. That is why you make entry-level pay. Unless you have demonstrated expertise with references to back it up, you'll have to accept starting out at the bottom.

Inexperience can be turned into an opportunity if you find the right customer to work with. If you're enthusiastic and willing to learn, many people out there would love to teach you. Seek out customers you can assist, and let them know you'd like to grow your skills. For example, if you're interested in being a photographer, look for temporary grunt work with a professional. During busy times such as late-summer senior pictures, many photographers could use an extra hand and help setting up. Once you're in the door and have proven you are a good worker, let your client know you are interested in more hands-on work. Learning while you earn from an experienced adult can be more valuable than a paycheck.

WARNING!

Work-related scams are everywhere, both in newspaper classifieds and online. You've probably seen the ads promising you will "Earn $1000s just by working a few hours from home." These are not legitimate business offerings and are only a way to trick you out of your money. *Chapter 8 will go into detail about avoiding these scams.* For now, just remember that if it sounds like easy money, it's probably too good to be true.

Finding Someone to Pay You

As you are forming your job plan, start considering who will actually pay you for this work. Remember that people are willing to pay for almost anything. If they think you can make their lives easier, if they see your product or service as unique, or if they have jobs they can't handle, they will hire you. You need to identify the job, spread the word that you can help, and follow through on your promises. In many cases, people might not even know they need you until you tell them. Remember that you also don't have to pack your day with work time. Working a few hours per week might be enough to meet your goals.

Start thinking now about your reasons for working. Of course, earning money is nice, but the right job with a good mentor has value because you'll be able to learn new things or build on your existing skills. You also might not need to earn a lot of money to meet your goals. If you only need to fill your tank with gas, you probably can get by with a one-time lawn mowing or babysitting job. On the flipside, if you're trying to build up a substantial chunk of money to put toward college, you'll need to develop a longer-term and extensive job plan. Identifying your objectives for working will help you set realistic goals and design a reasonable work plan to meet them. *Chapter 8 will cover goal setting and will help you create short- and long-term plans for making and saving money.*

Problem = Opportunity

To find customers, practice being observant, and think outside the box. Look around your neighborhood, your school, and among the adults you and your parents know. What areas of their lives could you help? Problems, changes, or needs in their lives equal ways to make money in yours. That doesn't mean you are taking advantage of them — many adults realize it makes more sense to hire someone to do easy chores than take time from their lives to do it themselves. Many times the person who pays you might not be the person you're working with.

For example, if you're running a sports mini-camp, you'll be working with kids, but their parents are the decision makers and pay the bills. Naturally, you'll have to interest the kids in your services, but ultimately, you need to convince mom and dad to hire you.

Everyone is a potential customer; even your parents or friends' parents might be willing to pay for extra work that needs to be done. You would be surprised by how many adults would kill for just two hours of help around the house, with technology, or with their kids every weekend. Just think how much you could make by filling this one need for families in your neighborhood.

Sometimes it can be difficult to know where the line between helping someone out and getting paid falls. Many times the job you are proposing to take on will be considered a "volunteer" position, especially because you are an inexperienced teenager. You'll have to be assertive and convey — respectfully, of course — that you're skilled enough to do the job, and you do expect to be paid for your time. However, it is OK to offer your services occasionally as a "charitable donation" as a way to get your foot in the door. Also, don't get greedy and start charging your friends and neighbors for things you would normally do for free. For example, if you have always watered the flowers while your neighbors are away, it would be wrong to start charging them now. However, if you've established yourself as reliable through this watering, you could turn this reliability into more paid work around their house.

CASE STUDY: ON THE JOB WITH JUSTIN KRELL

Occupation: Owner and
operator, Prairie View Cattle
Company and Krell Auction
Age: Started his business at age 13
jdkrell@jacks.sdstate.edu

Justin Krell at work on the farm. Photo courtesy of Justin Krell.

My great-great grandfather started our family farm in 1912. I am the fifth generation to grow up here, and at age 13, I decided to start raising beef cattle on my own. I began with one beef heifer and one beef steer purchased with money I'd saved from gifts and from showing livestock at the county fair. My dad and grandpa let me use some of our farm's equipment and feed to get started. When I eventually made money, I put the profits back into my business to purchase more cows and equipment.

I began to see the success other producers were having with Black Angus beef, so I decided to target that specialty market. So at the young age of 14, I borrowed $18,000 from the local bank to purchase 12 registered Black Angus bred heifers. Around this time, I found that feed costs were skyrocketing, so I decided to start growing my own feed, and I rented 50 acres of farmland from my great uncle. I was then able to raise my own feed and make extra revenue by selling the extra. I put this revenue back into my operation and used it to pay for advertising, and by 2011, my herd had expanded to more than 70 head of cattle. My original investment was earned back within five years.

The profit margins in the beef cattle business are historically very narrow, so I saw that I'd have to find a way to make my operation more profitable. For years, my dad had been selling direct-to-consumer, even if it was just friends and family, and he mentioned to me that this could work for an overall beef operation. I researched it and decided to start selling my beef directly to local consumers through an area sales barn. This cut down on the middleman costs, which increased my profit margins.

I also lined up a meat processor so the consumers could specify exactly how they wanted their beef cut up. Consumers found a benefit with this method because they knew exactly where their meat was coming from, and they saved nearly 10 to 20 percent on their grocery meat budget. In addition, I found that some of my customers only wanted a quarter- or half-beef, so I invested in a chest freezer and found a meat processor that was federally inspected, so I could legally sell beef by the retail pound versus in bulk. This increased my sales tremendously and has helped me to widen my customer base.

Word quickly spread through our community about my product, and I supplemented this with advertising on a local radio station and in our area newspapers. I also donated an average of 400 pounds of beef each year to local fundraisers. This was a great way to show the community that I cared, but I also found that the people who received the donated beef became customers later on.

In addition to Prairie View Cattle Company, I started Krell Auction Service in 2009. I graduated from auctioneer school at the World Wide College of Auctioneering and became a licensed auctioneer able to conduct any type of auction sale. I specialize in annual livestock sales of pigs and sheep and am looking to expand to estate, farm retirement sales, and eventually land sales.

My self-employment has taught me so much, including responsibility, how to manage my money, how to identify profitable markets, how to manage my time, and how to deal with people and provide customer service. It has also allowed me to pay for my entire college education, so I'll graduate without any student loans. Of course, it was hard work, especially on those cold, dark nights when the cows were calving and I knew I had to go to school the next day. I also think at times I was probably making an "hourly" wage that was below minimum wage, but I built a business with real equity, and overall I'm sure I made more than most kids my age.

Words of Wisdom: When you have an idea, run with it, and don't be afraid to fail. If you have determination in yourself, you will succeed. Remember, too, that you get out what you put in.

Combine your services

You've probably heard of bundling as it relates to computer games or cell phones, but this concept also is a perfect fit for the self-employed. If you've identified numerous but related areas you want to work in, find ways to offer all of these services to the same customer. When you're on the job, look for opportunities to "upsell" your range of services. For instance, if you're backing up someone's computer data, offer to clean up their MP3 files or organize their digital photo library (for an additional fee, of course). You don't have to be pushy or a high-pressure salesperson to make upselling work. In many cases, your customer might not even know they need your service or that you're capable of handling the work. If they are happy with your first work for them, you most likely will be given more work.

VOCAB

Upselling is used by sellers to add on related services or products to your purchase such as asking if you'd like to buy dessert with dinner. The thought behind upselling is the customer is already in the store with his or her wallet ready, and it is easier to increase this sale than to find a new customer.

Another great bundler idea is to bundle many customers together for the same service. This works great for dog walkers or child care. Instead of going to someone's house to babysit one child, set up a drop-in service to watch two or three kids of the same age from different families. The parents will love the free time, the kids will get to play with others their own age, and you will be getting paid three times the money. *Ideas for combining services will be included with the job listings in the following chapters.*

Make money off the busy season

Workloads ebb and flow during certain times of the year, and capitalizing on the busy season is a great way for the independent worker to make money. Caterers get swamped during spring graduation seasons, winterizing shops get busy in the fall, vacationers look for help during the summer — the list goes on and on and covers every sector of employment. Think about the busy seasons that relate to the job you'd like to do. Maybe you're great at food preparation and could offer up assistance to people hosting graduation parties. Maybe you love to decorate and could help homeowners doll up their houses for the holiday. Again, your job is to help people solve their problems, and all you need to do is identify that problem.

This busy season need doesn't apply only to individuals. Many regular employers also hire subcontractors during their peak times to help fill in gaps. This, again, often falls around big holidays, seasonal changes, immovable deadlines such as tax filing dates (April 15), or other big events in your community. *An outline for creating a independent-worker contract is included in Appendix A.* Just consider what unique skills you have that could be in demand during others' busy seasons.

Taking the next step

Succeeding at your job takes more than planning and motivation. Running even a small part-time operation will require administrative duties such as filing taxes and keeping records. Finding new customers will take some creative advertising and outreach to potential clients. Nailing down the job will take some good interviewing and negotiating skills. Keeping customers will require keeping your skills at top level and providing great customer service. Don't worry; you don't have to know everything to make money. Do some online research in your chosen job field to learn more specifics. Most important, ask questions if you don't know or understand what you need to do. Your parents are probably thrilled that you are getting a job of any kind and will be more than happy to help you. They even might be willing to fund your startup.

Foreword to Chapters 3 through 7

The following five chapters will offer you hundreds of ideas for making money. The descriptions will list information about each type of job including how it matches up with your interests, how much you can expect to make, and what kind of skills you need to succeed. Reviewing these highlights will help you decide if this job is right for you. Each job might have things you like and things you dislike. Take notes as you read, and don't dismiss every job based on the pay scale. Each heading will have related subsets that can be refined even further based on your experience. Think in small, manageable chunks to design your own employment. Use your notes and interests inventory to make your own job hybrid idea — you can combine a love of many things into one or two jobs that work for you. Remember, if you can find a way to meet someone's need, you'll find a way to make money. For example: the heading "Digital Photo Management" doesn't mean taking on one family's entire digital library. Instead, offer a service in which you name the digital files in each folder and make sure copies are printed.

The jobs listed in the next chapters aren't exclusive to the world of self-employment; they just lend themselves more easily to working independently. Many teens start out with a small self-directed job and find that they really enjoy it or dislike it intensely. This then leads to some direction for college, which can end in a career choice based on the work you did back in 11th grade. At this point in your life, none of these jobs have to be a lifetime commitment, just a way to make money that fits into your schedule and is not boring beyond all belief.

VOCAB

Gross income is the money you take in before any expenses or taxes are taken out. **Net income** is the amount of money left after taxes and expenses are deducted.

The wages and hourly rate data is taken from the U. S. Bureau of Labor's September 2011 projections. These are based on the national average wages earned in each of these categories, which means entry-level workers should expect to be paid less and highly skilled or experienced workers should expect to make more. Just because the average wage is a certain amount doesn't mean you'll be paid that much in your area. Many factors affect the going rate including your location, your skill level, your experience, and your competition. In addition, if you offer a specialized or unique product or service, you can charge more than average. If it's hard to find, it's worth more. This data is included here as a guideline to help you set your wages and determine if you really can make as much or more money by working on your own. In some instances, you might make less doing the job as an independent. *Details on assessing your competition and setting your price will be covered in Chapter 8.*

TIP!

As of 2011, minimum wage for most businesses is $7.25 per hour but this varies by state and industry. So, if you get a regular job, this is the least you can be paid before taxes. For information on your state's minimum wage laws, visit **www.dol.gov/whd/minwage/america.htm** and click on your state.

Another note about reviewing these wage statistics: These are the industry averages, which means the before-tax wages paid to employees of companies in these sectors. Unlike these employees, your wages will have to cover all related expenses of doing business.

Tom's Bike Courier Service

As an employee of a messenger service: Before tax wages = $192/ week; $2304/year.

Tom will be paid an average wage of $16 per hour, and he plans to work approximately three hours per day, four days of the week. All he has to do is show up to work, get his deliveries for the day, do the job accurately, and pick up his paycheck every two weeks.

As a self-employed courier: Before tax wages or gross income = $250/ week; $3000/year; $2700/year after expenses.

Tom is going to charge $25 per package, which includes pickup and delivery within a two-mile range. He estimates he should be able to make ten deliveries per week. His expenses include a bike, repairs, and advertising (estimated to be a total of approximately $300 per year). Tom will have to handle placing advertising, arranging deliveries, and collecting payment from customers.

From this example, you can see that Tom will make nearly $400 more per year by working for himself. However, his taxes might be slightly higher than when working for someone else, and he has to put in non-billable hours for the extras related to doing business. Assessing your idea in this way will help you decide if it is worth the extra effort. *Chapter 8 will explain how to determine if your business idea is worthwhile and profitable.* Like Tom, you'll have to consider these sorts of logistics and requirements needed to get the job done. With this information, you can calculate the true costs of doing business and determine what your net hourly rate will be. Hundreds of specific industry salary calculators are available online — just search for "average wages or pay rate" for your specific job. Although it's considered slightly rude to ask how much someone makes, you can probably get away with asking friends or trusted adults about their wages. Don't forget your parents, too, as they have experience in the work world and can help you decide on setting a fair price.

Now, let's get out the notepad and highlighter and find you a job.

CHAPTER THREE

Computer and Tech-Savvy Jobs

You might not realize it, but your generation has a special place in history as it relates to technology. Most of the communication technology we depend on today has only been around for 20 years or so. You are part of the first generation to come of age in an era with smart phones, the Internet, digital recording and photography, MP3 players, social networking, electronic readers, PowerPoint®, YouTube®, Facebook, and laptop computers. It's hard for you to even imagine this, but before you were born, your parents listened to music on their CD players — the iPod® did not exist. Because you've grown up with this technology, you've learned it as you grew, and unlike many adults, you aren't intimidated by the possibilities.

You can assume most people over the age of 40 are overwhelmed by their technology, either because they don't know how to use it, or they know how to use it but don't have time to manage it. This disconnect with technology is even more severe with your grandparents' generation. Most people are trying to stay on top of technological advancements as they relate to their job or home life. You, however, have known this stuff since you were a toddler. Even a minimal grasp of technology can be turned into a job adults are willing to pay for. Break it down into small chunks, and you'll make money off this sector.

Job Category: Computer Genius

If you're handy with computers and the Internet, this is the job for you. Many older people — maybe even your own parents — do not understand how to operate, update, or use the software on their

computers. Some don't even know how to delete email, send pictures, or browse through websites and would love help from someone who knows his or her way around a computer. Ask your parents right now, and they'll probably admit they need to back up files, clean up cookies, and generally get their computer, files, and programs better organized.

Potential hourly price range: You can expect to charge approximately $15 to $20 per hour. On-call and emergency technical services can be billed at $30 to $40 per hour.

Equipment or supplies needed: If you're working from home, you'll need a computer (preferably a laptop) and all related software, hardware, and connection cords. Depending on the type of work you are doing, you might need a printer, modem, router, Internet access, digital camera, or specialized software. When you are at someone's home or office, use their equipment and software.

Costs: Low if working offsite, high if using your own equipment

Logistical considerations: Insurance coverage might be needed if you are using a lot of expensive equipment. Check with your parents to see if this is covered under their homeowner's insurance policy. Transportation of yourself and your equipment to your customer's site

Permits/licenses needed: Minimal, might need software licenses

Skills and education needed: You will need knowledge of various computer types, functions, and formats. Depending on the type of work you're doing, you might need specialized programming skills or other technical know-how.

Fits with these interests and attributes: Computer and technical knowledge, problem-solving skills, good attention to detail, likes to help others, independent work-style

Your customer's profile:

Personal: People who are too busy to deal with overloaded and outdated computer files, those who need help learning how to use their computers, and those overwhelmed by their workload. Even your classmates might be willing to pay for assistance. Providing even a few hours of help can be life-saving to those up against a deadline or unexpected problems.

Business: Every business in your community, local nonprofits such as 4-H or your church, and even your school can benefit from expert assistance with their computer systems. Small businesses, such as your local main street bakery, are too busy running their business to deal with setting up a website. Medium-sized businesses and nonprofits are struggling to keep up with demand and probably don't have someone on staff who knows computers well. Large businesses encounter overload during their busy seasons and would love an extra set of hands to take over Web-page maintenance or data processing. Do not forget other computer professionals in your area who might be looking for independent contractors to help them out on occasion. *Check Appendix B for a list of websites with secure payment structures and scam-free systems for finding these types of jobs online.*

References needed: Yes, but minimal — your work will prove your value.

Seasonality: Any time of the year

Safety issues: Loss of data (yours or your customers), damage to equipment or software if work is done improperly, personal safety issues related working alone or with strangers

Marketing ideas and how to reach your potential customers: Spread the word among the adults you know and on social networking sites. Many nonprofits, such as your church, could use help creating a website. Offer to do a small job to prove you know what you are doing, then ask for more work, or request a referral. Put up a flyer in your local grocery store that reminds people they need to protect their computers, precious documents, expensive music libraries, and pictures. Offer holiday specials such as "Give your parents the gift of music. Hire me to organize their music library or create a special playlist for their anniversary."

Build in special offers and package deals or create group sessions: Each of your customers probably needs any of the following breakdowns. Talk with them about their needs and make suggestions for what they should do. For example, if you're hired to update a security program, offer to do an extra job of deleting cookies and potential threats on their computers. Much of the instruction-based jobs are perfect for group sessions. For example, set up a Saturday morning training session for four or five customers at once, and you'll make four times the money for that hour.

Break it down and make it your own:

▸ **Computer tutoring (the basics such as email, Internet surfing, downloading, etc.)**

▸ **Software instruction (especially common programs such as Excel®, PowerPoint, and Word®)**

If you have the patience to deal with beginners, you can find endless work teaching people the basics of using their computers, the Internet, and easy software programs. For personal and work reasons, adults of all ages are trying to stay up-to-date with computer technology, but many lack even a basic understanding of how to work their equipment. Ask your grandparents, and they can probably name five things they would like to learn how to do. You most likely already know all of this and can offer a tutoring service that helps them along.

▸ **Software installation, maintenance, and updating**

Maintaining current software, choosing new programs, or installing these programs is another area many people are afraid to tackle. Helping people with proper installation and maintenance is an easy job for you and gives you a foot-in-the-door for more extensive work.

▸ **Security and virus protection installation and maintenance**

Offering to keep security systems up-to-date, doing periodic scans, and teaching people about basic computer security measures is another easy job that gives you a chance to garner more work from the same client.

▸ **Computer cleanup or data backup service**

Many people don't realize how easily their computers can crash and permanently delete all the files, pictures, and email they have accumulated. In addition, surfing the Web leaves cookies that clog up the works and slow down the computer's speed. Offer a service — weekly or monthly is best — to clean up your customer's computer and back up their important data. This is a great way to develop repeat customers and a guaranteed income.

▸ Computer repair and file recovery

This is for the customer who didn't hire you to do backup. If you're especially talented with the inner workings of a computer, you can offer a file recovery service or general repair service of computers, printers, scanners, and other equipment. Offer your clients a guarantee, so they know they will only have to pay if you get the job done. Be sure you can fix it before you take on work, or you might end up losing a few hours without pay.

▸ Computer software development

▸ Application (or app) developer for smart phones or tablets such as the iPad®

You can make a lot of money in this segment, but it requires a high level of programming expertise and can take a lot of time to develop. For example, the iPhone® app process can take more than a year before you're approved to sell your product. If you identify even the most basic need and create a program to meet the need, you can make money in this area. Who knows? You might develop the next "Angry Birds®."

▸ Software, app, video game, or website testing (sometimes called beta-testing)

As a beta-tester, you will field test or review other people's programs, websites, video games, or apps before they are released to a wider market. Most of these jobs are directed by the developer or the company trying to market the product, and you'll be given clear and concise directions for your testing. Your review and suggestions will be passed on to the programmer to improve the product. Finding these jobs can take a bit of online research, but once you've done well on one job, the company will continue to offer you freelance work.

▸ **Website, social network page, or blog creation and maintenance**

▸ **Online auction listing creation and maintenance (such as eBay® or Etsy®)**

▸ **Word processing, data entry, or transcription**

Most small businesses know they need an Internet presence to do business, but setting up a website is time-consuming and overwhelming to those unfamiliar with computers. Numerous online services make creating Web pages simple. You can be the hero to that small business and have fun creating a website or blog. Once those pages are created, they will need regular updating and maintenance. If you are the "administrator," you now have a regular income and can work from any location. Additionally, during busy seasons, nearly every business needs help with data entry or simple word processing. Many of these jobs can be found online. *See Appendix B for listings.*

▸ **Internet researcher (for products, travel, services, or work-related issues)**

This is another area in which people need help because they don't have time to do it themselves or don't know how to go about it. Often, writers or grad students also need an extra pair of eyes to search out information online or fact check the data they've found. Through school, you've probably gained a lot of experience in how to use the Web effectively. This is also a great stepping-stone to research- or writing-oriented future careers.

▸ **Organizing existing digital music libraries (i.e. making sure all songs have titles)**

▸ **Downloading new music from CDs or online music stores**

▸ **Creating playlists from this music**

You might not agree with your parents' choice in music, but they've probably switched over to using an MP3 player and amassed a sizable digital music collection. Because their favorite music was around before iPods, a good chunk of their music is probably still on CD or even LP records. And once those CDs are downloaded, many of the titles and track information does not show. This is a great job for someone like you. With an intimate knowledge of iTunes® and other music organizing programs, you could offer a custom playlist service in which you create playlists based on your customer's input.

▸ **Taking online surveys or joining online focus groups**

Many sites have popped up now that do customer surveys for large companies. They bring the proposed product or packaging to you through short online surveys, and you tell them what you think. You will have to give them a bit of personal information — many require you to be 18 or older — and they'll send you regular links to surveys. Often, you'll receive free products or gift cards in exchange for your participation. Be wary of scams, though, and never pay to participate or give out your personal information — all they need to know is your age and gender. *Listings for online surveys are included in Appendix B.*

Job Category: Technology Assistant

This job is similar to helping with computers but focuses on the other technologies we handle in our daily lives. From smart phones to GPS systems to programmable TV remotes, complicated technology is everywhere. Many adults feel overwhelmed, not because they can't understand how to use it but because they are too strapped for time to learn how to use these technologies to make life easier. People are paying big bucks to upgrade their phones but only use them to check email. Televisions, new cars, electronic readers, and even refrigerators are being sold with bonus techno-features that  most never bother to try. Even the latest MP3 player has updates that take time to learn. You can help — just find your niche and use the knowledge you already have to make some money.

Potential hourly price range: You can expect to charge approximately $10 per hour for the basics and $15 per hour for more advanced devices. On-call and emergency technical services can be billed at $20 per hour

Equipment or supplies needed: You'll be working in other people's homes with their equipment and will most likely only need a simple tool kit for attaching wires or replacing batteries. Your own personal laptop or smart phone might be handy if you need to access instruction manuals online or call the manufacturer's helpline. You also might need a small stepstool for placing components on higher shelves. Special equipment is needed for transferring home movies and can be purchased at most electronic stores or found at large copy stores. A scanner is also nice for copying old photos but can also be done for a fee at a copy store.

Costs: Zero for work done onsite, minimal if purchasing a scanner, high if buying movie conversion equipment. Check at your local library or research inexpensive retail alternatives such as FedEx® copy centers for inexpensive options.

Logistical considerations: Insurance coverage might be needed if you're using a lot of expensive equipment. Check with your parents to see if this is covered under their homeowner's insurance policy. Transportation of yourself and your equipment to your customer's site

Permits/licenses needed: Minimal — might need software licenses

Skills/education needed: This will depend on the type of work you're doing. For example, to offer photo management service, you'll need an expert understanding of photo management software and websites. Much of this knowledge can be attained quickly through the product's website or instruction manuals. Choose an area to work in that you're familiar with or are willing to learn quickly. You want to spend your time earning money, not reading technical manuals.

Fits with these interests and attributes: Interested and knowledgeable in technology and the latest equipment, problem-solving skills, good attention to detail, ability to communicate and define problems through customer discussions, independent work-style, good organizational skills

Your customer's profile:

Personal: Anyone with an electronic device that has many features, requires frequent upgrades, or that holds a lot of files or information. Many of these people know they need to get organized but don't have the time — or the expertise — to deal with it.

Businesses: Similar to the personal customer, business owners also deal with lots of technology that is supposed to "make life easier," but they don't want to take time out of their busy day to read a manual. This is especially true for small business owners who need to focus on the paying customer. Offering a little training or assistance to these folks can garner you a lot of business.

References needed: Yes, but minimal — your work will prove your value.

Seasonality: Any time of the year but especially after the big holidays when people get these types of devices as presents

Safety issues: Loss of data or irreplaceable items such as family photos. Take precautions when handling these types of materials. Potential damage to expensive electronics if installed or updated incorrectly, in addition to the simple fact that you're dealing with fragile equipment that will break if dropped or mishandled. Also, the inherent personal safety issues when you're working alone or with strangers

Marketing ideas and how to reach your potential customers: Similar to the computer-related marketing ideas, your first course of marketing is to spread the word. Tell your friends' parents, your parents, and your neighbors you're willing to help them with the mundane technological issues they are facing. Remind them that their digital photos or music files are expensive to replace — if they can even be replaced — and it's worth a little money to gain some piece of mind. Offer a "monthly cleanup" service in which you review their devices and make downloads, uploads, or deletions as needed. Encourage them to get the most out of their expensive technology by learning all the intricacies available on each device, and show them how you can make it easy to learn. Consider making up a flyer advertising your assistance, and hang it up in stores where people buy electronics.

Build in special offers and package deals or create group sessions: This segment is tailor-made for a holiday special. New TVs, MP3 players, and cell phones will fill the holiday boxes, but then someone has to hook them all up and learn how to use them. Offer a "holiday" special in which you help pick out the right equipment, come to their house to help install it, and teach everyone how to use these new toys.

Break it down and make it your own:

▸ Electronic reader instruction and organization

These devices go by many names including Kindle® or Nook®, and new devices are coming to market every year. They are simple and straightforward to use but also have many advanced functions many people don't use to the fullest. Offer a simple lesson or monthly service to keep things running smoothly.

▸ Cell phone/PDA instruction and syncing (basic or advanced)

▸ GPS updating/instructions

Everyone thinks they need a smart phone or advanced global positioning system, but many still just use the basic functions or avoid updating the device altogether. You can help with this simple task and get the job done in no time.

▸ Gamer system setup

If there is one area in which teens are absolute experts, it is the video game sector. Now you can finally put all those hours of practice into making some money. From old-school PlayStation® games to the newest Xbox online setups, many adults want to get into the game but don't know where to start. If they don't have a resident teen, they have to depend on store clerks to help them. You can offer assistance in system purchasing — great for moms looking for Christmas presents for the first-timer. You can help hook everything up, give basic game-playing tips, and help more experienced gamers tweak their systems or layout their playing area.

▸ **Digital photo management**

The digital photo world has exploded over the last ten years. Adults have kept up in this area — at least when it comes to buying equipment and taking pictures. The problems crop up with downloading these pictures and managing the photo library. Every photo needs a tag, most need cropping or color fixing, and some just need to be deleted. However, this time-consuming task often is put off, and then the job is just too big to handle. Ironically, these photos are often considered a family's most prized possession. This is where you can step in and help without needing lots of technical know-how. This job can be divided and combined in numerous ways:

- Downloading photos to personal computers or to an online service
- Backing up existing photo files
- Tagging and organizing downloaded photos
- Cropping or fixing downloaded photos
- Printing off downloaded photos or transferring them to disc
- Filing, labeling, and organizing printed photos
- Scanning and transferring printed photos to digital format
- Digital camera instructions
- Downloading old home movies or transferring them to digital format

▸ **Home electronics assistant**

As with digital cameras, people have readily adopted and happily purchased the latest in-home electronic equipment. When it comes to using these devices to their fullest, though, things get confusing. A brand new HD and DVR system with a shiny, button-filled remote is nice to unwrap, but what happens next? You can step in with your expertise to hook everything up, make sure all the functions are working (even that blinking 12:00 is gone), and teach your customer how to use all the features. After all, you don't want to spend thousands of dollars on a new device and then only be able to channel surf. Here are a few ways to break this job down:

- Connecting new components to existing system
- Instructions on use of new devices (such as DVR)
- Programming new devices or remote controls
- Troubleshooting when things do not work
- Monthly cleanup of DVR shows or setting DVR recording schedules

▸ Equipment refurbishment or disposal

Once you've helped your customer replace his old equipment, he might want to get rid of it. You can help with disposal in numerous ways.

1. If it still works, you could help sell the equipment by listing it online such as on Craigslist (**www.craigslist.org**).

2. If it's broken and you're handy with electronics, you could try fixing it for your customer or for resale. You also could take what parts are still working to save for future repairs.

3. If it's broken and beyond repair, you could haul it away for them. You'll have to pay a disposal fee, so be sure to include this in your charge.

Are the ideas flowing now? Can you see how even the smallest tech-related job can reap you a big payday? Just within your parents' circle of friends are probably a dozen people who would hire you to perform simple but time-consuming tasks or teach them the basics of their technology. Many people do not realize how easy it is to learn to use their devices — especially with a non-threatening expert like you helping them. You only need to identify that need, create your solution, and spread the word that you can help get it done.

CHAPTER FOUR

Make Money with Your Hobbies and Interests

Your favorite activities, interests, and hobbies don't have to be shut away while you are earning money. If you love it, if you're good at it, and if you're willing to expand on your skill base, you'll be able to make money at it. Best of all, doing what you love will make the day go by quickly, and getting paid for this work is an added bonus. Any interest or hobby has the potential to be a moneymaker. There are three ways to make money through your hobbies:

1. Going on your own. For instance, if you love to bake cookies or make jam, you could sell your products at your local farmers market.

2. Finding someone else to hire you to do the work. An example would be turning your love of interior decorating into a moneymaking venture by offering to help homeowners decorate for the holidays or set tables for a special occasion.

3. Finding someone more experienced than you. For example, if you love carpentry work, you could find a general contractor who needs a temporary assistant. While you're working with him, let him know you'd like to broaden your skills and learn more advanced carpentry techniques.

The sky really is the limit when you think creatively about finding ways to use your hobbies. As mentioned earlier, breaking down your idea into pieces will help you manage your workload. Think in small bits to take on work — preferably jobs that can be completed in just a few hours versus over the course of a week. You'll be paid sooner, and you will not be tempted to take on more than you can handle.

Job Category: Tour Guide

Do you know your way around your city, neighborhood, or the outlying countryside? Use this knowledge to make money by offering tour guide service to visitors or new residents of your community. The tours do not have to be your standard "walk around the city" tour. You could offer special activities such as a mini-fishing trip, historical or offbeat landmark tour, or a short wildlife or bird-watching excursion.

Potential hourly price range: You can expect to charge approximately $10 per hour, per person.

Equipment or supplies needed: You only need a good pair of walking shoes, appropriate clothing, sunscreen, and a guidebook. For large tour groups, it might be necessary to carry a handheld microphone or loudspeaker so your voice will carry. If you are doing a specialized tour, such as a bird-watching tour or a ghost tour, you might need appropriate equipment: binoculars, costumes, etc.

Costs: Zero if your customers provide transportation, minimal cost of apparel (which you have anyway), high cost if you are driving the tour.

Logistical considerations: Limited equipment needs, but you might need to have printed handouts with information about your tour. You will have to provide a large vehicle and proper insurance if providing transportation.

Permits/licenses needed: Driver's license if providing transportation. Check with your state codes regarding passenger allowances for your age. Your city or tour location might also require a tour guide permit or license to operate. Be sure to check into this well in advance as the permitting process can take some time to complete. *Chapter 10 goes into detail regarding researching and securing specialized licenses and permits.*

Skills/education needed: This will depend on the type of work you're doing. Growing up in the area might give you enough knowledge to provide a full tour. Review popular guidebooks for more information or to see what most people are looking for in a paid tour.

Fits with these interests an attributes: Must have excellent communication, public speaking, and people skills, patience to answer the same questions over and over, enthusiasm and high-energy, good organizational skills. Personality is everything when giving tours.

Your customer's profile:

Personal: People visiting the area looking for something fun and offbeat to do or new and current residents of your community who want to learn more about the area

Businesses: Larger businesses that host out-of-town colleagues or clients often try to set up short non-work-related activities for these folks while they are in town.

References needed: Yes, but minimal. Word-of-mouth is key here.

Seasonality: Year-round, but it might get busier in areas where summer is considered "peak" season or during holidays when people have visitors.

Safety issues: Personal safety of yourself when working with strangers, safety of customers if doing strenuous activities. Learning CPR is good for everyone but especially if you're going to be working with the public in this capacity.

Marketing ideas and how to reach your potential customers: Spread the word through social networking sites related to your area as many have their own tourism pages or blogs. Let your neighbors know your offering this service and talk with the people at your local tourism office or city hall. Consider getting an ad in printed visitor guides for your area — this can be expensive, but these guides stay on the shelves for a long time.

Build in special offers and package deals or create group sessions: Offer a small memento of the tour such as a badge or sticker. Offer successive tours where people can earn points or medals to trade for a T-shirt (with your tour guide name and number, of course.) Offer two-for-one specials or free tours for referrals. Partner with sites you will be visiting — such as restaurants along the route — to offer a free cup of coffee to your tour participants.

Break it down and make it your own:

Your tour doesn't have to be an all-encompassing guide to the city. Think of the places you like to go, the things you like to do, or what you would like to see when you are traveling. People who have these same interests also will want to be shown around the city when they come to visit. Make your tour as interesting and informative as possible. Consider wearing a costume, putting together a printed summary, or offering souvenirs. Research as much as possible, and be sure to point out unique or unusual features, such as historically significant buildings or locally specific wildlife. Here are just a few ideas for putting together a tour:

- Biking, hiking, or rock-climbing tours
- Birding or wildlife viewing tour
- Geocaching tour
- Child-focused tours (which are also a great addition to a babysitting service)
- Restaurant, coffeehouse, or independent music venue tours
- Garden or public art tours
- Geographic, historical, or unique tours
- Architectural tours or a symbol scavenger hunt through the city
- Holiday decorations tour — outside or inside
- Haunted house or ghost tours centered around local legends

Job Category: Music, Instrumental, or Vocal

Some people are blessed with musical talent. If you are one of the blessed or just know a lot about music, beginners of all ages would love your help. If you like to perform, you can also make a nice self-employed living from singing at events or getting gigs for your band. And if you are ambitious, you can try putting out your own music CD and hope to go big time.

Potential hourly price range: The income amount ranges wildly here depending on where you're working and what type of work you're doing. Basic music lessons can be charged at $15 to $20 per hour. Musical performance can range from $50 to $500+ per appearance, and self-published CDs can garner you anywhere from nothing to a lot of money.

Equipment or supplies needed:

   Costs: Minimal for singing, high if purchasing instruments, costumes, performance gear, or booking studio time

   Logistical considerations: You'll need a properly functioning instrument and a space to practice or give lessons, transportation for you and your equipment to and from your performances, and a phone so clients can reach you for bookings. You might have to work weekends, as this is when most bookings occur. You also might need performance equipment such as microphones and costumes or nice clothing for event appearances.

Permits/licenses needed: None

Skills/education needed: You'll need advanced musical skills in your chosen instrument. You'll need to be able to read music and be able to teach others how to read music. If self-publishing your music, you'll need to know how to use equipment and software designed for that purpose.

Fits with these interests and attributes: Musical interest and excellent grasp of the subject, stage presence, ability to work with people, good time management skills, professionalism, and patience for teaching

Your customer's profile:

Personal: People who want to learn how to play an instrument, read music, or improve their singing voice, or advanced musicians who need an accompanist. This also includes parents who want to help their kids learn to play or sing. Your customer is also the person looking for musical talent for their special event, such as a wedding singer or a holiday party.

Businesses: The main business customer you'll have is the venue or event organizer looking to book a musician or group of musicians for an event. This is not limited to bars. Many public places such as museums, parks, and community functions like to have background music or a featured performer.

References needed: Minimal, but it's recommended that you have a "reel" or a recorded version of your performances.

Seasonality: Year-round but might peak during holidays

Safety issues: Personal safety when working alone, in unfamiliar surroundings, or late at night

Marketing ideas and how to reach your potential customers: Word-of-mouth is your No. 1 asset when looking for new gigs. Play wherever and whenever you can — even if it's in your own backyard — until you get the buzz going about your music. Spread the word to people you know are planning big events. Tell your band or choir teacher you'd like to give lessons, so he can send new students your way. Record yourself performing and post to social networking sites. Never miss a talent show; even if you don't win, you'll still get some great exposure. Hang fliers advertising your lessons at local music stores.

Build in special offers and package deals or create group sessions: Offer to be the "warm-up" band and help the main band set up. Find other music teachers in your area who might have overflow and offer to help them. Team up with other music teachers and set up a recital for your students. Chances are someone in the audience will be interested in hiring you for their own children.

Break it down and make it your own:

In addition to teaching others and performing music yourself, these are some fun ways to be involved in music by helping others:

▸ Setting up a home music studio

Besides needing lessons for play, your customers need help purchasing the right equipment and getting it set up in their own home. From music stands to expensive keyboards, you can help them find the right piece for their goals and teach them how to use it.

▸ Creating original music

Have you ever tried writing music? Many bands and performing musicians search for original pieces to add to their repertoire. You can also make good money from writing jingles or short pieces of music for advertising companies or websites. Be sure to retain rights to your written pieces and keep track of who is buying your originals. *Appendix B lists a few websites for finding song writing work.*

▸ Music camp

In addition to private lessons, you can also set up mini-music camps for kids in your area. Parents who want their kids to learn music also need things for them to do during school breaks. They would be thrilled to send them to you for a few hours, and you can charge per kid, per hour. Just be sure you have enough instruments, space, and patience to accommodate everyone. Be sure to put on a mini-show at the end for the parents to see what their kids were working on during the camp.

Job Category: Photography or Videography

People love to have posed or artistic photos of their kids, pets, and special events, but a trip to a professional photographer can be expensive. Luckily, the price of digital equipment and the ease of developing these photos is within reach of just about anyone. All you need is the eye for composing a good picture and the patience to get your shot.

Potential hourly price range: You can expect to charge approximately $12 per hour for the basics and $20+ per hour for more advanced services such as artistic compositions. Full event photography such as bar mitzvahs can be charged at a "per project" price and can range from a few hundred dollars into the thousands.

Equipment or supplies needed: You'll need a good camera (preferably digital) with a zoom lens and the capability to capture fast motion, a tripod for your camera, backdrops and lighting for portraits, access to scenic locations, a good microphone for event videography, and a computer with Internet access for downloading, editing, and developing film.

Costs: Zero if you can borrow equipment, high if you purchase equipment.

Logistical considerations: Transportation to events, equipment maintenance, equipment storage sites, and adequate insurance coverage for your equipment. You'll also have certain time considerations for long events or portrait sittings. Any event or art photography will require permission from the subjects.

Permits/licenses needed: None

Skills/education needed: Depending on the scope of work you intend to do, you can take on many photography jobs with a basic, beginner's understanding. However, more advanced photocomposition skills or developing experience can lead to higher wages.

Fits with these interests and attributes: Interest in artistic and technical aspects of photography, good attention to detail, ability to communicate with people and accept constructive criticism, be able to follow directions, and handle stressful situations.

Your customer's profile:

Personal: Your primary customers will be looking to get portrait-type pictures or have events documented through photo or video. You can also sell your original photos as artwork through craft fairs, art shows, or online sales sites.

Businesses: Some businesspeople require portraits for work reasons, and nonprofits, government agencies, media outlets, or regular businesses need event photography. Media outlets looking for current event photos and clip art services will often buy rights to your photography to resell online.

References needed: Minimal but will need a portfolio of your past work. Self-directed pieces are acceptable.

Seasonality: Year-round but might spike during big holidays or local events

Safety issues: Personal safety when working with strangers especially during large gatherings, potential for loss of irreplaceable "photo opportunities" if your equipment fails, issues with chemicals if you are developing film yourself

Marketing ideas and how to reach your potential customers: Your No. 1 advantage in this field is that you'll be cheaper than any standard photography service. This can help you but also make people wary of hiring you. Having a good collection of referrals and a well-rounded portfolio will help ease these fears. Social networking is the best way to market yourself. Additionally, meet with large catering centers or event planners near you to see if they need help with photography or would keep your name on file.

Build in special offers and package deals or create group sessions: Offer add-ons whenever possible such as "Order one 8-by-10, and I'll throw in two 5 by 7 prints." Group packages are perfect here, especially for portraiture. For example, if you're taking kids' pictures, why not encourage the grandparents to come by for an additional family portrait? You are already there, and it will take little extra work to get additional business. Make it easy for your customer to order more. You also can offer finishing services such as framing or special album collections.

Break it down and make it your own:

▸ Standard portraiture

You have sat for your own portrait many times over the years, so you know how this goes. All you need is a stool, chair, or location for your subject to sit or stand. Be sure you have proper lighting, try lots of poses, and take plenty of shots. This is not just for children or people — remember grandparents, families, pets, and even favorite vehicles.

▸ Event photography

People love to document personal milestones such as baptisms, weddings, and graduations with video and photos but often want someone else to take the photos so they do not miss the event. This sector of photography can earn you a lot of money but also can be quite time-consuming and stressful. Remember that your customer is depending on you to record this once-in-a-lifetime event, which leaves no room for error. A great add-on service you can offer here is to edit the video with music and artistic framing to create a special memory for your client.

▸ Art photography

Photos also can become beautiful artwork that people would love to hang in their homes. Browse the aisles of any home décor store, and you'll see hundreds of photos selling for big bucks. Let your creativity flow — even an up-close shot of a flower petal can be artistic when printed in large scale. Consider learning how to matte and frame your photos, and they'll sell for more. You are creating one-of-a-kind artwork, so be sure to sign all your photos. A great place to sell your pictures is at local craft fairs or through online sites such as Etsy. You can also sell your original photos to clip art services that will then license these pictures out for other use. *See Appendix B for leads on photography websites.*

▸ Photojournalism

Similar to staged event photography, you can use your camera to document newsworthy events as they happen in your community. These do not have to be earth-shattering occurrences and can be community gatherings, church events, school activities, or anything else your friends and neighbors would be interested in. Couple your photos with descriptive captions and a well-written article, and you're a reporter. Sometimes called a "stringer" by newspapers, most photojournalists contract for work on an as-needed basis. Be sure to ask your editor for specific guidelines for photos, and always get permission from the subjects in your photos. Once the photos are taken and accepted by your editor, you'll be paid. If you happen to document an important happening that affects a broader audience, your piece might be placed in regional or national publications, and you should be paid more or at least retain copyright to the photo. *Refer to Chapter 10 for more information on these legal aspects.*

Job Category: Artistic Expression

Similar to art photography, you can sell your original artistic creations to just about anyone. People scour art fairs, craft shows, and online sites for original art for their homes, offices, or for spaces they've been hired to decorate. Many people look for "up and coming artists" just like you to buy some of their first pieces with the hope that someday you'll make it big and that first art piece will become quite valuable. Others like to commission original artwork and look for young artists with a fresh eye. Artwork is not only paintings; it can include any medium. Even metal jewelry or hand-painted dinner plates are considered artistic in many circles.

VOCAB

Commissioned work means someone hires you to create artwork based on their subject matter or specifications. For example, you could be hired to paint a portrait of Fluffy, your neighbor's prized poodle.

Lesson No. 1: Always, always, always sign your artwork and take digital photos to document your pieces. Lesson No. 2: Keep a record with the name, address, and phone number of people who buy your pieces, so you know where they are and you can use this person as a reference. This will not only help you build a portfolio but will help you keep track of your pieces for future reference.

Potential hourly price range: This is not really an "hourly wage" type of job, and the range is wide. You could create the next Mona Lisa and make millions or carry around a stack of line drawings that never sell. Browse the aisles of a local craft fair, visit a retail art gallery, or search online sites such as Etsy for pieces in your chosen medium. For commissioned pieces, estimate your time needed for sittings, finishing, and framing, and charge at least $20 per hour. Retain reproduction rights to your work, and never work free unless you control the piece until sale, such as in a consignment gallery.

Equipment or supplies needed:

Costs: Minimal if working with paint, high if special equipment such as a kiln is needed. Join an artists' co-op or local community college for large equipment needs such as a pottery wheel.

Logistical considerations: In addition to your particular medium's equipment needs, you'll need adequate space for creating the art, storing pieces while they are drying or in progress, for meeting with clients for sittings, and for displaying your finished product. You'll need a computer and digital camera for listing pieces online. You'll need transportation and a display system if selling your artwork offsite.

Permits/licenses needed: None

Skills/education needed: Depends greatly on the type of work you're doing, but art is subjective. If you like it and can find someone else who also likes it, you can make money. Some rudimentary education is needed for using potentially dangerous materials such as a welding torch or glass cutters. Classes are often available through your local community education offices.

Fits with these interests and attributes: Artistic inclination, creative thinking, self-motivated, able to take constructive criticism, people skills for dealing with clients or gallery owners

Your customer's profile:

Personal: Anyone looking for original art. Commission clients are often the same people who would hire someone to take a photo but are willing to pay more and wait longer for the finished product.

Businesses: Creative-minded businesses such as advertising agencies love to use original art in their workplace. Many interior decorators are looking for artwork to go with their client's designs or for temporary home staging needs.

References needed: None for original creations. Clients looking for commissioned work will want to talk with previous clients or look at your past work or portfolio.

Seasonality: Year-round

Safety issues: Personal safety if using dangerous materials or working with heavy objects. Take the necessary precautions such as wearing gloves or safety goggles.

Marketing ideas and how to reach your potential customers: The best way to reach your customers is to get them to see your work. Show your friends and your friends' parents, put a few pieces in local craft consignment shops, post pictures on social networking sites or online sales outlets such as Etsy, and set up shop at a few art fairs. Enter art competitions held through your school, local fairs, or other organizations. Look online for contests in your medium. *Appendix B lists some good websites to review.*

VOCAB

A **consignment store** is a business where people bring goods to sell such as artwork, antiques, or secondhand pieces. The owners handle all the aspects of doing business including the physical store, advertising, staff, and so on. The store then takes a percentage off the sale amount of your item to cover its costs. Depending on the store, you'll either be paid immediately when you bring in the item or after the item is sold. Some stores have a time limit for sales, and you'll be asked to retrieve your item if it doesn't sell.

Build in special offers and package deals or create group sessions: Some businesses don't have the money to purchase art outright. Offer to rent out your artwork for a few months at a time, with the option to buy, of course. Realtors, home stagers, and speculative builders are also a great market for art rental, especially during their busy open house seasons or local "tour of homes," held in the spring. Be sure to have your name and contact information prominently displayed with the artwork to reach potential customers.

Break it down and make it your own

In addition to creating artwork to sell on your own or by commission, you can also use your artistic abilities to help others learn your chosen medium. These include:

▸ Art lessons or assistance in setting up a home studio

Many older adults take on new hobbies in their retirement. These people love the energy and excitement of a young person like you and would be excellent students. You'll most likely have to provide some of the materials, but you could also assist these people in buying the right materials to create their own at-home studios.

▸ Large-scale painting such as murals

You don't have to be a "tagger" to create larger-than-life artwork. Many people now are installing large artwork to cover an entire wall, especially in nurseries or children's playrooms. You can create your own artwork or find templates or stencils that help you decorate an entire room with just a paintbrush and a few cans of paint.

▸ Art camps

This is a great "bundle" idea that works perfectly during your spring or summer break from school. Create a half-day, mini-art camp for elementary kids where you can teach them the basics of art. You'll have to provide materials — just build this into the cost of the camp. You might also have to supply a space to work in, but you could also offer to come in for a couple hours to local day cares and work there. Parents will love this distraction for their kids, and you'll probably have a lot of fun teaching. This is also a great way to find new clients (i.e. the parents) to buy your original artwork.

‣ Graphic design

Artistic talent has a place in the world of advertising. Every ad, website, product label, and logoed T-shirt has been created by a graphic designer. Many beginning graphic design jobs can be found on sites such as Elance® (**www.elance.com**) and offer higher pay than most art-related jobs. However, artistic work done as a graphic designer becomes the property of the client. Consider teaming up with a friend who can do the writing, and you can offer a team to your clients.

CASE STUDY: ON THE JOB WITH REILLY NEWMAN

Occupation: Graphic Designer
and CEO of Zangaroo Designs
Age: Started his business at age 16
reilly@zangaroodesigns.com
www.zangaroodesigns.com

I started my graphic design firm, Zangaroo Designs, when I was 16 years old and a sophomore in high school. Back then, I was told I had talent in graphic design, so I invested time into studying the field and practicing my skill. I decided to work for myself because I wanted to provide honest, pure, and specialized graphic designs. I also wanted to challenge myself and see just how far I could push myself and my dreams. My first job was creating my own ads and producing designs for my high school. Word began to spread, and I knew I had a success on my hands.

I then used my social network and friends to keep the buzz going, and my company has grown because of this support. I also made T-shirts right away with my name and logo on them — these were a huge, unexpected hit that also splashed my name all over town. I took my initial profits and invested them into buying a better computer and the tools I needed to really excel at my profession. That investment has paid off, and I now have both local and international clients and have designed logos, posters, business cards, signs, and attire.

I've learned a few things along the way that have helped me grow my business. Lesson No. 1 is to keep good records. I save invoices, receipts, and anything else that seems important, and then I create tables to log sales and clients. This is not the most exciting part of my job, but it is great for business. Lesson No. 2 is to not take things too personally. People will have criticism about your product or business; that does not mean they are criticizing you as a person.

Words of Wisdom: Never let someone look down on you because of your age, and if they do, you don't want to work with them anyway.

Job Category: Writing

More writing outlets are available now than ever before, and more people looking are for writers to do freelance work. From blog writing to Web page copy to newspaper articles to self-published books, if you have writing ability, you can make money. Many are looking, too, for the "young voice" to speak for your generation.

TIP!

Save copies of every finished piece you sell. Be sure to record who bought it, how much it sold for, and where and when it was published. If possible, ask your publisher for a digital file of the finished piece, and save it for your portfolio.

Potential hourly price range: As with original art, the range for writing fees is broad. Basic, for-hire writing such as blogs, newsletters, or journalistic writing can be charged at $10 to $15 per hour. More advanced writing with detailed research needs can be billed at $20 to $25 per hour. Book writing is paid on a per-project basis, and payment depends on your experience, the subject matter, and the length of the book. Many people choose to self-publish their own books, but this can require large up-front costs with no guarantee of getting back your investment.

Equipment or supplies needed:

Costs: Zero to minimal for basic writing, high if self-publishing a book.

Logistical considerations: You'll need a computer with an Internet connection and a printer. You'll need a good memory drive or recordable CDs to save backup copies of your work. You'll also need access to research materials, but most of these can be ordered through your library. You might need transportation if you are going out on interviews or to cover events.

Permits/licenses needed: None, but you might need a "press pass" for reporting.

Skills/education needed: You must have good grammar and excellent writing ability. You'll need to know and follow writing styles appropriate to your chosen outlet, such as AP Style. Guides to these styles are available online. You'll need advanced research skills and to cite your sources. You'll have to be able to accept editor's comments and make necessary changes. You might need interviewing skills.

Fits with these interests and attributes: Critical and creative thinking abilities, interest in language and writing, independent work-style, good organizational and research skills, ability to meet deadlines

Your customer's profile:

Personal: Most writing business is limited to business customers. However, you can find personal customers who will hire you to write for them (i.e. ghostwriting) or who will buy your finished book.

Businesses: Businesses of every size and in nearly every sector have the need for freelance writers. From news outlets to marketing companies to book publishers to private businesses, thousands of opportunities are out there for writers.

References needed: Yes, but minimal. Keeping a portfolio of past work — even school writing projects — will help you in the door.

Seasonality: Year-round

Safety issues: If on assignment or at an interview, you'll be alone with strangers or in an unfamiliar place. You could also reveal too much personal information in your writing. Be especially careful with online writing to not give out private data about yourself or the subjects you are writing about.

Marketing ideas and how to reach your potential customers: Many freelance writers today find work through online resources such as Elance and iFreelance (**www.ifreelance.com**). People looking for writers go to these sites and post the details on the job they need done. Writers then bid on the jobs and are awarded the job through the website. You can find some interesting work through these sites, and it is a great way to build your portfolio and experience base. Be careful, though, because there are many scams out there. Do not pay to find jobs, do not give your personal contact information to people you do not know, and look for sites that have some sort of moderator to help you deal with problems. *See Appendix B for more writers' websites that offer secure payment structures and scam-free systems for finding clients.*

You also can find writing work by spreading the word to the adults you know or by visiting local businesses. Even small retail stores can benefit from a brochure, newsletter, or newspaper ad. Offer to take on these jobs, and you can gain some good experience and more customers.

Build in special offers and package deals or create group sessions: Do you have a friend with artistic or photography skills? Try teaming up to provide graphic design services or photos to go along with your writing. Offer a group package to small businesses. For instance, give your local florist a year's worth of newsletter ideas on the seasons and important flower-giving holidays. Offer to help a local nonprofit with press releases or small writing jobs — just be sure to get published credit so potential clients see your work.

Break it down and make it your own

No matter what type of writing you're doing, be sure you understand how you'll be credited when the piece is published. If you're ghostwriting or creating advertising, you most likely will not get credit, and your work can be altered or reused without your permission. Even if you won't receive a byline, ask your client if you're allowed to use the piece in your portfolio or if he or she can be used a reference.

VOCAB

Often used for biographies or scientific writing, a **ghostwriter** is someone who writes or significantly rewrites a piece for someone else because that person knows the subject well but isn't a good writer. Ghostwriters aren't given author credit or recognized in the finished work.

▶ Journalistic or informative writing

Outlets such as magazines, newspapers, and online news sites all are looking for that next big story or detailed articles for specific interest groups. From dog groomers to home interiors to fishing enthusiasts, there's a place for every topic. The key as a freelancer is to find the buyer for your idea. After you get some experience and a few bylines under your belt, editors might start contacting you. Until then, there are two ways to find work:

1. At the development stage: Most publishers know for months in advance what general topics will be placed in upcoming issues. The articles often already are outlined and sourced; they just need someone to pull it together and write it. They will post these topics through online sites or on their own website and look for submissions from interested writers. Your submission should include a sample of your writing (not on the posted topic), why you are qualified for this job, ideas on how you will approach the topic, and the fee you want to get. Never write an article on "spec" or send in a "sample" article. Sadly, unscrupulous people will take your sample and print it without paying you or giving you credit.

VOCAB

Writing "**on spec**" refers to doing work "on speculation" in which you complete the piece without an up-front commitment for payment. If the client likes the work, you'll be paid.

---

2. At the proposal stage, sometimes called a query: These are articles you develop; you submit the idea to a media outlet. For example, you could propose the idea for an article about tips for applying to college and submit this idea to magazines aimed at that audience. You don't need to submit the entire article; send in your outline and summary of the article, the opening paragraph, and information on why you should be selected. Look online or at your local library for more information on submission guidelines and query writing. Check out *How to Write a Query Letter: Everything You Need to Know Explained Simply*, also by Atlantic Publishing.

TIP!

A true writer uses his or her own words. Never lift copy and use it as your own. Paraphrase it, and then write it again before you use it or plan to give your source full credit. Most editors now run writing through copy-checking programs, and any plagiarized copy will be rejected — along with your job and your reputation.

▸ Marketing or advertising writing

This type of writing is everything related to advertising for product sales, business services, events and entertainment, and even political or social ideas. Marketing includes: newspaper ads, billboards, television and radio commercials, brochures, newsletters, blogs, tweets, social network updates, and so on. Many of the large writing jobs such as TV commercials are handled by big ad agencies, but smaller jobs such as product blogging or small business brochures can be handled by a freelancer. Ask local stores if you can help them, and look at the previously listed writing sites for posted jobs. Again, don't do work free, on spec, or as a sample. Offer to revise and edit until the customer is satisfied before you expect payment. *Appendix B lists good websites for finding this type of freelance work.*

▸ Short story, poetry, nonfiction, or fiction writing

Do you have the next *Twilight* saga in your head just waiting to get out on paper? Writing a novel is a huge undertaking, and you might have to wait a long time to get paid. This does not mean, though, that you shouldn't pursue your dream of writing a novel. While you are working on your book, you also can find less intense writing tasks that offer faster payment and the possibility to become a published writer. As with magazine writing, you can write a short book or a downloadable e-book around any informative topic. Poetry and short stories are published in numerous compilations and online sites. All you need to do is find the publisher. You also can submit your writing to contests. You might not win, but you'll get your name seen and your work read. Check the Writer's Digest website (**www.writersdigest.com**) and magazine for links and information about publishers and contests.

▶ Editing, proofreading, and writing assistance

Good writers depend on an editor and proofreader to help them out and make their work better. If you have excellent grammar skills, good attention to detail, and the ability to deliver constructive criticism, this is a great way to make money. College campuses are a great place to find customers, as many students are looking for proofreaders at term-paper time. If you're skilled at writing, you can also offer your help to make others' papers better. Remember, you're not writing the paper, just offering suggestions for improvement. *Editing jobs are also listed on most of freelance websites listed in Appendix B.*

▶ Writing customized children's books or family histories

This is a fun way to use your creative skills and make a child happy. Write up a simple fairy tale with at least one boy and one girl character and find free illustrations or ask a friend to draw some pictures (for a fee, of course.) Using simple publisher's software or templates you find online, you should be able to plug in the child's name for each character and print out a book in which they are the star of the story.

Many families, too, would love a written account of their family history. This doesn't have to be a genealogical record but could be compiled from short interviews with family members. Sometimes the day-to-day details are the most interesting part of a family's life, and you could help record this for future generations to look back on.

Job Category: Interior Decorating or Interior Design

When you walk into a house, do you notice the paint color and fabric choices first? Do you run through room layouts and arrangements in your head? You'd probably love being an interior designer. A full-time decorator, of course, has a college degree and his or her own office, but there's plenty of room for a freelancer to tackle this job or help a busy designer. You can assist in everything related to home design including: picking out furniture and laying it out in the room, designing and purchasing décor to outfit a mantel, faux finishing walls with a paint treatment, or even helping people find the perfect pillow to match the sofa. For from-scratch designs, your customers will expect you to provide them with complete details, swatches, clippings, drawings, cost estimates, and timelines for the work schedule.

Potential hourly price range: You can expect to charge approximately $10 per hour as a designer's assistant and up to $25 per hour for original design work.

Equipment or supplies needed:

Costs: Minimal for basic designs, high if you're doing the actual work such as painting

Logistical considerations: You'll need basic measuring tools such as a tape measure, ladder, tool kit, and a level. More advanced decorating will require tools such as painting gear, power tools, or moving gear. You'll need transportation to your client's home and to the stores for supplies. An Internet connection, computer, and phone are essential for tracking down price estimates, putting designs together, and arranging deliveries. Have a digital camera for taking before and after pictures

Permits/licenses needed: None

Skills/education needed: Formal education is not necessary, but know the basic principles of design. Check your local library for books on basic interior design. You'll need to stay current with design trends by reading magazines, searching online, or through watching home decorating shows. You'll need drawing or drafting skills to show your plan on paper. You'll also have to know — or have access to — cost estimates for the materials you use.

Fits with these interests and attributes: Creative thinking and problem-solving skills, good attention to detail, ability to communicate and define problems through customer discussions, people-handling skills for dealing with movers and painters — or a tough customer — independent work-style, ability to meet deadlines and budgets

Your customer's profile:

Personal: Your primary customers will be homeowners looking for small decorating assistance. For instance, a new parent decorating a nursery or someone trying to spruce up the family room doesn't want to pay expensive rates to a professional designer. He or she will appreciate your assistance if he or she has confidence in your abilities.

Businesses: Few businesses care about interior designing their spaces, and those that do rely on big firms. Realtors and home stagers, though, could use an assistant during the busy spring open-house season. You probably won't get a lot of original design work, but it's a great way to show off your skills, which could lead to more advanced work.

References needed: Minimal, your portfolio and design sketches will speak for themselves

Seasonality: Year-round, but might peak a few months before big holidays such as Christmas or spring events such as graduation or open houses

Safety issues: Personal safety when working alone, with strangers, handling power tools, lifting heavy furniture, or climbing up and down ladders; potential to damage client's property or possessions during the work stage

Marketing ideas and how to reach your potential customers: Spread the word to the adults you know, especially those involved with real estate or new home construction. Post before and after pictures to social networking sites showing off the designs you have done — even if it's your own room. Ask your parents to let you decorate a part of your home and take pictures to put in a portfolio. Put up a flyer advertising your help during the busy season. Enter your decorations (with your parents' permission) into "Parade of Homes" type events in your area. Be sure to display your name and hand out business cards, so people know you did the design.

Build in special offers and package deals or create group sessions: Offer an added bonus to people who hire you, such as a piece of your original artwork or a photo album documenting the redesign. Be creative and find cool pieces or wall treatments only you can provide. Offer a satisfaction guarantee for all your work, and don't expect payment until the work is done.

Break it down and make it your own

Think of all the small areas in a home that need to be decorated or changed with the holidays or special occasions. Every one of these spaces or holiday updates makes the perfect job, will fill your portfolio with great photos, and can open the door to larger projects. Here are just a few ideas to get you thinking:

- Baby's room or children's playroom decor
- Game room, family room, or home-entertainment spaces design
- Hand-painted wall designs or stenciled quotes
- Photo or art search for the client — based on subject matter or color
- Create a photo wall of framed family photos
- Personal décor shopper — can be as specific as looking for an antique buffet
- Holiday mantel design or tablescapes for dinner parties
- Feng shui consultant
- Outdoor space design such as decks or patios

Job Category: Cooking and Food Preparation

Job description: Do you love preparing a meal or trying out new dishes? Do you have a secret family recipe, a holiday specialty, or just love to cook for others? During busy holiday, wedding, and graduation seasons, people are always looking for a kitchen assistant or someone to help them with their workloads. Many hosts, too, love to find unique menu offerings, so if you have a special dish only you know how to make, you practically can set your own price. *Chapter 7 will cover how to cook or bake products for sale.* This section will focus on cooking for hire either as a personal chef, kitchen assistant, or instructor.

Potential hourly price range: You can expect to charge $10 to $15 per hour for basic kitchen assistance, $20 to $25 per hour for personal chef work, and $25+ per hour for specialty items. Cooks also often receive a 15 percent tip at the end of an event.

Costs: Low if working off site, high if using your own equipment

Logistical considerations: If working from your own kitchen, you'll need all the necessary equipment for preparing, cooking, warming, and serving your dishes. You'll also need a dependable vehicle large enough to transport your products. You might need a uniform or nice clothes for working upscale events.

Permits/licenses needed: None if working in a private home or for a catering service, but you might need a food license if preparing food in your home for sale. Check with your local extension office or your state's department of health for more information.

Skills and education needed: If your food tastes good, you need no more training. It is necessary, however, to have knowledge of basic food handling safety rules. This goes beyond hand washing and includes heating and cooling recommendations, allergy awareness, and even current food recall alerts. The government site at foodsafety.gov (**www.foodsafety.gov**) covers every food-related topic you'll come across and is a great place to check if you have questions. Depending on what type of food you're preparing, you might also need to know specifics on kitchen equipment or specialized ingredients.

Fits with these interests and attributes: Ability to work with a wide range of people and give direction, ability to handle stressful situations while under a time-crunch, time-management skills, problem-solving and planning skills, good attention to detail, like to help others, independent work-style

Your customer's profile:

Personal: People looking for a cook to prepare and serve an entire meal, but this meal can be everything from a small sit-down dinner to a full wedding banquet. Your customer also can be the person who wants to handle the cooking but needs a kitchen assistant to help with preparation stages, such as chopping veggies or watching times on things in the oven (this is sometimes referred to as a "sous chef.")

Business: Businesses hire caterers to provide food for corporate events, so you most likely will not find a lot of work through this avenue. However, you can find cook's assistant work during busy holiday seasons.

References needed: Minimal — your food will speak for itself.

Seasonality: Any time of the year but especially busy during holidays, wedding and graduation seasons, and local events

Safety issues: Personal safety issues related to working alone, with strangers, and with hot kitchen equipment. The belongings of your customer can be damaged if you spill food or have a fire while cooking. Customer health is also an issue if food is prepared improperly.

Marketing ideas and how to reach your potential customers: A great way to market yourself is to provide free samples of your specialty. Consider going door-to-door (to homes you know) with a mini-plate of what you can cook. If you know an adult with an upcoming event, offer your assistance in the kitchen. Spread the word through social networks, and be sure to take pictures of the meals or events you've prepared, even if it's in your own home. Carry business cards with you, and consider having aprons, hats, or shirts printed with your name — potential customers might be on the guest list. Talk with area caterers and event venues such as golf courses or restaurants, and let them know you're available to fill in on an as-needed basis.

Build in special offers and package deals or create group sessions: Consider keeping a few trustworthy friends on standby so you can also offer waiter service for the events you are catering. Connect with local women's groups or community education offices to offer a group cooking class.

Break it down and make it your own

▸ Holiday or event kitchen helper

Many hosts love to prepare food for their guests, but the workload becomes overwhelming. Whether it is frosting Christmas cookies or preparing a thousand mints for graduation, you can step in as a valuable assistant to take the pressure off and get the job done. This is also a great opportunity to prove your worth in the kitchen, which can lead to more extensive cooking jobs for the same customer.

▸ Ethnic specialty chef or instructor

You might have grown up making latkes, tortillas, or lefse from scratch, but these are unique, delicious, and mysterious to those outside your ethnic group. Many people would love to serve these at their parties or learn how to make them at home — just be sure you aren't sharing any family secrets.

▸ General cooking lessons or cooking camp

Believe it or not, many adults can barely boil water. Simple kitchen dishes such as homemade macaroni and cheese, pot roast, or soup are easy to teach, require simple equipment, and can be covered in less than an hour. Offer group sessions for adults or kids in which you teach the preparation of a couple different dishes to make a meal you can then share at the end of the session. You could also offer a class focused on variations of one specific item such as Christmas cookies or appetizers — set up a few stations with three or four items, and when you're finished, everyone goes home with a plate of everything. Look for a community kitchen space or set up your class through your local community education office so you'll have a space big enough for your group.

▶ Menu planning

All great cooks have files and files of recipes and cookbooks they are dying to try. Now is your chance to put these recipes to good use by helping others plan their meals. You could offer a weekly service that includes meal planning, an ingredients shopping list, and preparation. You can also offer special event menus based on your customer's needs — after a few events, you'll have a nice menu collection you can use over and over again.

Job Category: Athletics

Do you play "organized" sports in school or as an extracurricular activity? If you're playing at a varsity level or have recognized success in this sport, you can turn these skills into a great part-time job. Now that you're at the top of your game, you can use your experience to help teach the next generation of players.

Potential hourly price range: You can expect to charge approximately $10 to $15 per hour, per pupil, but these rates range widely depending on the sport. More advanced training for physically demanding sports can earn more per hour. Camps or group sessions can be charged by the day — typically $50 to $100, per student, per day.

Equipment or supplies needed: If you're working from home or hosting a camp, you'll need all the necessary equipment for your sport. You'll also

need facilities such as a playing field to host the camp. You can expect —
and it is OK to ask — your students to bring their own gear.

Costs: Low if working offsite and with others' equipment, high if using
your own equipment or providing a practice space. If you need a playing
field, check with your community education office for rental options and
build this fee into your price.

Logistical considerations: Your equipment might get more wear and
tear. You'll also need a vehicle to transport gear.

Permits/licenses needed: None.

Skills and education needed: You'll need advanced knowledge in the
mechanics and equipment needs of your chosen sport. Know basic first
aid for the inevitable bumps and scrapes that occur with physical activity.
Advanced first aid is also a good idea if you're participating in more
injury-prone sports such as football or hockey.

Fits with these interests and attributes: Excellent communication and
people skills, a fondness or at least tolerance of children, an understanding
of the basics of the sport, patience to answer the same questions over and
over, enthusiasm for teaching, and good organizational skills. Personality is
everything when teaching others.

Your customer's profile:

Personal: Your primary client probably will be older elementary or
middle school children — but your true customers are these kids' parents.
The kids will have a few years of early elementary sports experience, and
their parents are looking for ways to improve their skills. For example, a
preteen baseball player wants to learn more about pitching before trying out
for his summer traveling team, so he asks his dad to hire a pitching coach

for lessons. His dad looks into hiring a professional trainer and finds the fee to be outrageous. You as a varsity player have the skills but charge a lot less, so dad hires you to help his son. Of course, the son is thrilled because you are probably someone he already looks up to. Some sports, such as golf or bowling, also attract older players, those who have taken up the sport later in life and want to learn the finer points or improve their game.

Business: You might be able to offer your services to personal trainers or coaches to help fill in during extra busy times.

References needed: Yes, you can use your successes such as a varsity letter or tournament accomplishments. Word-of-mouth is key here.

Seasonality: Any time of the year, and it depends on your particular sport.

Safety issues: Because of the physical nature of your sport, you have some serious safety issues to consider. Your personal safety can be compromised due to working with strangers, and you could injure yourself while you're playing. Use proper technique and avoid doing the same motion over and over. Make sure you understand and know how to teach proper technique, and be careful not to push your customers too far — especially young children or those who are out of shape. You might also be dealing with young children who require direct and constant supervision. Choose locations where the kids are kept in with fencing, so they cannot run off or dart into a street. Never cut corners — be sure to have safety gear and adequate hydration for every client, every time.

Marketing ideas and how to reach your potential customers: As mentioned, word-of-mouth is essential, and the best way to spread the word is to start networking with places that provide gear, training, or practice space to potential clients. For example, if you'd like to give running lessons, talk with the workers at a running shoe store or post a flier in their lobby. You can also spread the word at your school and through your coaches that you would like to coach younger kids. If you play for a well-recognized coach or team, you can use this as an added bonus to clients.

Build in special offers and package deals or create group sessions: If possible, arrange for your clients to watch your games and offer a postgame picture or field time. Offer a repeat customer discount or a reduced rate when parents sign up more than one child.

Ways to break it down and make it your own

The primary way to make money is to work with beginners. You don't need to teach them every nuance of the sport. Just a few lessons or suggestions for improvement are enough for most people. Any sport will work for this category, but here are the easiest sports to turn into lessons or day camps:

- Football
- Volleyball
- Baseball and softball
- Basketball
- Hockey
- Soccer
- Lacrosse
- Golf
- Tennis
- Bowling
- Swimming or diving
- Wrestling
- Cheerleading, gymnastics, or danceline

> ### TIP!
> Be sure to check with your coach to make sure you aren't breaking any league rules by participating in your sport out of season or with other coaches. This can be an issue in some high school leagues, and you do not want to affect your eligibility status.

▸ Gear shopping service

Your customer also might need help in purchasing gear to start out or in upgrading to more advanced equipment. If you have friends looking to get rid of their used gear, you could also help your customers connect with them.

▸ Day- or week-camps

In addition to private lessons, you can also set up mini-camps for kids in your area. These will be especially popular in the weeks right before the season starts or during school breaks when parents are looking for things to occupy their kids. Even just a few hours in the morning for drop-in lessons or circuit training is a great alternative for parents. You could also team up with other players on your team to offer a camp with two or three "training stations" for the kids to try out. The great part about camps is you can charge per attendee, so you earn your hourly rate for each kid that shows up. Make sure you have enough equipment, safety gear, space, and patience to accommodate everyone.

▸ Specific technique, safety, or "what not to do" training

With so many positions and techniques, the sport you play can be broken down into small parts that can then become the basis of a lesson. For example, softball pitchers are prone to shoulder injuries, so you could build an entire class on teaching correct form for release or motion. You could also teach kids safety issues related to the sport such as how to recognize and avoid concussions. Remember, small chunks can make you big bucks.

‣ Videography and clip assembly for tryouts

Many athletes dream of getting athletic scholarships or playing on elite teams in the off-season — but these dreams often require submitting a clip reel, resume, and coach recommendation package to college coaches or team athletic directors. If you know the sport well, you can help assemble these reels for other players by picking out their most fantastic plays and putting together their applications. If you have good connections in the sport, you could also act as a sort of matchmaker or agent to introduce your friends to potential coaches. Again, make sure you are not breaking any league rules.

Job Category: Outdoor Sports

These are the sports activities that do not fit into the high school organized sports model but require just as much physical ability and training to pursue. Whether it is fishing, kayaking, rock-climbing, or surfing, if you have fun doing it, plenty of others would like to try it.

Potential hourly price range: You can expect to charge approximately $15 to $20 per hour, but these rates range widely depending on the sport.

More advanced training for physically demanding sports can earn more per hour.

Equipment or supplies needed: The equipment needed depends on the individual pursuit, and you most likely already have what you need. You can also expect your customers to have their own gear or be willing to purchase it before working with you. Instruction manuals or guides are nice to have on hand to refer to or hand out to clients. You'll most likely need transportation to get to the site, but this might also be available by riding along with your customer.

Costs: Low unless you need to provide equipment

Logistical considerations: Your equipment might get more wear and tear than usual, and you might have to keep replacement parts on hand.

Permits/licenses needed: Minimal, unless the sport you are participating in requires one, such as a fishing license. Be sure to inform your customers ahead of time if they will need a license and give them information on where they can purchase it.

Skills and education needed: You'll need advanced knowledge in the mechanics and equipment needs of your chosen sport. You'll also need knowledge of good places for beginners to learn — for example, a ski hill suited to beginning snowboarders. Know basic first aid for the inevitable bumps and scrapes. Advanced first aid is also a good idea if you're participating in more dangerous sports such as rock-climbing, kayaking, or snowboarding.

Fits with these interests and attributes: You must have excellent communication and people skills, an understanding of the basics of the sport, patience to answer the same questions over and over, enthusiasm for teaching, and good organizational skills. Personality is everything when teaching others.

Your customer's profile:

Personal: These customers want to learn the sport or build on the basic knowledge they have. Your customer's age can range from small children up to retired people — and also can cover every age at once if you're teaching an entire family in one session.

Business: You might be able to provide a service to businesses that have out-of-town clients looking for an activity. You can also offer your services to established guides to help fill in during extra busy times.

References needed: Yes, word-of-mouth is key here.

Seasonality: Any time of the year, and it depends on your particular sport.

Safety issues: Personal safety issues related to working alone or with strangers and physical safety issues for you and your customers as they relate to your activity. Never cut corners here, and be sure to have safety gear, food, and hydration for every client, every time. Know all the laws related to your sport and follow them to the letter.

Marketing ideas and how to reach your potential customers: As mentioned, word-of-mouth is essential, and the best way to spread the word is to start networking with the places that provide gear to potential clients. For example, if you're a fishing guide, talk to people at area tackle shops. Be sure to post details of successful trips — with your customer's permission — to sport-related chat rooms or social networks. If you have a particularly successful day, send in the story with pictures to local papers and be sure to include your name as the guide. You can also consider buying ad space in newspapers and magazines, but this can get expensive.

Build in special offers and package deals or create group sessions: Partner with other businesses near your location to offer "free" service to your customers. For example, see if the ski lodge will give your customers a hot cocoa if you bring in a group during slow days. Offer your customers a souvenir (with your name printed on it), and consider giving discounts for repeat customers, referrals, or large groups. Take lots of pictures, and provide a link so customers can download their photos when they get home.

Break it down and make it your own:

The primary way to make money from your outdoor sports interests is to be a guide or an instructor for beginners. You don't have to provide an entire lifetime's worth of lessons or a three-day-long trip to succeed —a few hours are enough for most people. Some people just need an expert to help them buy the right gear. These hobbies lend themselves well to making money:

- Fishing, trapping, or hunting
- Hiking and orienteering
- Geocaching
- Camping and general outdoor survival training
- Rock climbing or mountaineering
- Skiing — cross-country or downhill
- Snowboarding
- Boating — canoes, kayaks, speedboats, sailboats
- Waterskiing or wakeboarding
- Surfing or windsurfing
- Ice skating
- Snorkeling or scuba diving

▸ Outfitting service

Your customers might also need help in purchasing their gear to start out. The choices are often overwhelming, and you can assist them in making the proper selections for beginning use. If you have friends in the sport looking to get rid of their used gear, you could also help your customers connect with them or help them evaluate used gear they are considering for purchase. Some people with more advanced skills might be planning trips that need outfitting — you can be their personal shopper and help them make selections based on your experience.

▸ Day- or week-camps

In addition to private lessons, you can also set up mini-camps for kids or adults in your area. During school breaks, parents are looking for fun activities for their kids, and families frequently like to learn new activities together while they are on vacation. You can charge "group rates," which means you make your hourly rate for each participant, and that can add up to big bucks. Make sure you have enough equipment, space, and patience to accommodate everyone.

▸ Fish and game cleaning and cooking

If you are in the fishing or hunting guide business, you can offer an additional service in which you clean the game for customers or teach them how to do it. You then can cook a wild game feed of what you have harvested or teach them how to prepare the dishes once they get home.

▸ Taxidermy service

Another fish and game tie-in is offering taxidermy services — you can do this yourself if you know how or offer to handle the arrangements needed to preserve their prized catch. There are also options now available for those who practice catch-and-release in which you only need a photo and measurements for the taxidermist to create a replica mount of your fish.

Job Category: Academics and Tutoring

You can make money at every level of tutoring from teaching the basics to working with advanced learners. If you have a thorough understanding of the subject and can impart this knowledge to others, you can be a tutor. Math, science, English, and composition are the most likely topics in which to find students, but don't forget the subjects outside of these areas. If your school offers the course, you can find students to work with. You can also earn money by teaching refresher courses to adults returning to college.

Potential hourly price range: You can expect to charge approximately $10 to $15 per hour, per pupil.

Equipment or supplies needed: You need minimal equipment and can use the textbooks you have from school. It will make work easier if you have access to a computer with Internet service so you can review subjects and check your answers. For basic tutoring, you might want flashcards, pens and paper, and small rewards such as stickers for children.

Costs: Zero if using what you have, low if buying textbooks and note pads.

Logistical considerations: You need either a quiet space to teach in or transportation to your student's home. Your student's study needs might conflict with your schedule if it falls during end-of-the-semester or finals time.

Permits/licenses needed: Minimal, might need software licenses for specific subjects.

Skills and education needed: You'll need thorough knowledge of the subject matter, but you must also understand the basics for beginning learners. You'll need to know what grade-appropriate goals are for your students. This information can be found online or by asking the parents of your pupils what they are working on in school.

Fits with these interests and attributes: You must have excellent communication and people skills, patience to deal with beginning learners, enthusiasm for teaching, positive attitude, and good organizational skills. Personality is everything when teaching others.

Your customer's profile:

Personal: Parents of kids who need help will be your typical customers. The age of your students, however, can range from young elementary kids to college-age. If the child is struggling in the subject and you can help, he's a customer. For advanced tutoring, you can also find adult customers such as those wanting to brush up on classes needed for college or work.

Business: Few businesses need tutors; however, you can offer your services to professional learning centers or other tutors to handle their overflow.

References needed: Yes, but minimal — your transcript and your work will prove your value.

Seasonality: Any time of the year, but your workload might peak near the end of school semesters or big test dates such as the ACT or SAT.

Safety issues: Personal safety issues related to working alone or with strangers. If you're working alone with young children, you'll also be responsible for their safety while they're in your care.

TIP!

Be careful to keep your client's information confidential. Don't talk about your students by name or discuss their grades or progress with anyone other than their parents or teachers.

Marketing ideas and how to reach your potential customers: Social networking will find you a lot of customers. Spread the word and ask your parents to tell their friends that you want to help. Tell the teachers and guidance counselors at local schools, and do not forget the elementary schools. Post fliers in local businesses where students frequent such as coffee shops, fast food restaurants, or popular hangouts.

Build in special offers and package deals or create group sessions: Offer special study groups to your previous or current students as finals approach. Give a family discount when parents sign up two or more children, or give your current students a "refer-a-friend" discount. Team up with friends to offer a group session with stations where kids can get tutoring in more than one subject. When putting groups together, pay attention to the skill levels of the students involved. If you have a wide gap in ages, you might need to put together more than one lesson plan to accommodate everyone.

Break it down and make it your own

▸ Specialized study groups

As you know, the end of the semester brings with it finals and that last chance to help your GPA. For middle school and high school students struggling with the topic, a weeknight or weekend study group can be essential. Set up a short two- or three-hour  session to review the semester's coursework and provide them with a sample test. Check with the teacher of each class for ideas and sample tests. Be sure to offer a break midway through the session with snacks and beverages. After the tests are over, turn these participants into regular customers by offering an ongoing study group.

▸ Mini-camps

As with the sports camps listed in the previous section, many parents look for children's day activities during school breaks. Many times, they send their kids to established "learning centers" such as Sylvan Learning®. You can offer a similar service and charge a substantially lower rate. In addition, the kids probably will have more fun with you. Just be sure you have enough books, paper, teaching space, and patience to accommodate everyone. You'll also need to give the kids an exercise and snack break every two hours or so. Consider teaming up with a few friends to offer a full day camp with tutoring and fun activities built in together.

CASE STUDY: ON THE JOB WITH IONNIE MCNEILL

Occupation: President,
The Baby Billionaire
Age: Started her business at age 15
ionniemcneill@yahoo.com
www.thebabybillionaire.com

Ionnie McNeill at school. Photo courtesy of
Ionnie McNeill.

I became self-employed by combining what I love to do with my desire to own my own business. In grade school, I learned how to invest in the stock market, and by age 10, I had my own portfolio of stocks and bonds. When I was old enough to get a "real" job, I started working part time as a way to fund my investments in a Roth IRA. By high school, I realized that people were willing to pay me to tell my story, inspire other students, and even teach them how to invest. It really was no-brainer — by speaking to others and teaching them about investing, I could get paid by doing what I love.

My business continued to grow through high school, and I found most of my customers through my speaking engagements. There always seemed to be someone in the audience who wanted to hire me for another speaking engagement. Therefore, repeat customers and word-of-mouth has been my business strategy since the beginning. I continue to give keynote speeches, offer workshop trainings, and host an annual Youth Investing Conference. This early start allowed me to grow my business to a point that now supports the lifestyle I want.

I will admit that I did receive some skepticism at first from friends and family. I didn't take offense to their caution because I realized that many of these skeptics didn't have an entrepreneurial outlook and didn't understand how it could all work out for me. I didn't brush off their criticism completely, though; instead, I used it to help me set realistic goals and thoroughly plan my business.

I believe that "teamwork makes the dream work," so I have been careful to choose colleagues that can add skills to my business. This experience has taught me how to work with different personalities, and I have learned that sometimes a working relationship just needs space to succeed. I have also been active in professional organizations such as the National Speaker's Association® and Better Investing®. These groups have been an excellent resource for my business — not only in developing my investment education but also in building my business through the contacts I have made.

Working for yourself is not really a nine-to-five job. This flexibility is one of the perks, but you often find yourself working after hours, on the weekend, and sometimes to the detriment of your personal life. When you love what you do it is easy to work a lot, but it is important to be careful to maintain a healthy balance in your life. Remember to take time out to have fun, too.

Words of Wisdom: Now is the best time to start your own business. The world is waiting for your solutions, inventions, and creations. Do not wait to make an impact — start now!

▶ College prep

If you live near a college — especially a two-year or community-type college — you can find opportunities to tutor college students. Sometimes college students are looking for a study partner to quiz them or help them work through small parts of their course loads. A great way to reach these customers is through social networking and by spreading the word to friends who have graduated and are now in college.

> **TIP!**
>
> Your job as a tutor is to *help* your students learn and improve their academic skills, not to give them the answers. Never share tests you've taken or papers you've written, and do not do their homework for them — this is cheating, and you both could get in big trouble.

Job Category: Foreign or Second Language Instruction

If your primary language is not English — but you have a good understanding of English — you can make good money through teaching others your first language, by helping native speakers learn English, or by providing translation or transcription services. You can also find work teaching English as a Second Language (ESL) courses. These courses are popular in areas with concentrations of new immigrants and places with a lot of foreign visitors and are frequently offered through community education or library seminars.

> **SIDEBAR**
>
> Do you know American Sign Language or ASL? This is considered a "second language" and counts toward high school or college language requirements. Courses in ASL have grown in popularity, and instructors are in demand. Many young parents are also teaching sign language to their babies as a way to help them communicate before they can talk. If you know ASL, your job options are wide open.

Potential hourly price range: You can expect to charge approximately $15 to $20 per hour. Some translation, transcription, or on-call services can be billed at higher rates — it depends on the language and the scope of work being completed.

Equipment or supplies needed: For ease of working, have a computer (preferably a laptop) with software related to the language you're teaching. You'll also need a chalkboard or dry-erase board for teaching, flashcards or memory devices, and textbooks or dictionaries with both languages.

Costs: Low unless buying a large quantity of textbooks or software.

Logistical considerations: For teaching in your own home, you will need a quiet space large enough to seat all your students with a method of demonstration such as a dry-erase board. If working elsewhere, you will need transportation to your client's location.

Permits/licenses needed: Minimal, might need software licenses. Some translators do need proper accreditation for legal documents and professional settings, such as when working in a medical facility.

Skills and education needed: You'll need thorough knowledge of the subject matter, but you must also understand the basics for beginning learners. Study the specifics, so you can teach it properly.

Fits with these interests and attributes: You must have excellent communication and people skills, patience to deal with beginning learners, enthusiasm for teaching, positive attitude, and good organizational skills. Personality is everything when teaching others.

Your customer's profile:

Personal: This is a diverse group because it covers everyone from parents who want their kids "immersed" in a language to adult travelers who want to know how to order dinner while on vacation. Your personal customers also can be those visiting or newly living in the United States — these people need to learn or improve their English — or fellow students who need tutoring in the language.

Business: Few businesses need language tutors. However, you can offer your services to those businesses that deal with international clients — you can offer translation, transcription, or act as a liaison with their foreign customers. Also, you sometimes can contract with your local library or community education office to offer a group language class. *Check Appendix B for a list of websites with secure payment structures and scam-free systems for finding transcription and translation jobs online.*

References needed: Yes, but minimal — your grasp of the language will show through.

Seasonality: Any time of the year

Safety issues: Personal safety issues related to with strangers — be especially aware of certain cultural differences such as women working with men. If you're working alone with young children, you'll be responsible for their safety while they're in your care.

Marketing ideas and how to reach your potential customers: Social networking and word-of-mouth is your best avenue to finding new customers. Spread the word at your church, community center, or school. Talk with the teachers, pastors, and social workers in your community to connect with new residents needing help with English. Post fliers (in both languages) at local businesses where students frequent, such as coffee shops, fast-food restaurants, or popular hangouts.

Build in special offers and package deals or create group sessions: Offer special study groups at local community centers and mix in cultural foods or customs while you're teaching. Organize a special celebration day unique to the country where your chosen language is spoken — for example, host a Cinco de Mayo celebration for those learning Spanish. Give a family discount when parents sign up two or more children, or give your current students a "refer-a-friend" discount.

Break it down and make it your own

▸ Specialized study groups

As with standard academic tutoring, if you're teaching a commonly taught foreign language such as French or Spanish, you can find students in your own high school or local college. Near the end of semesters when finals are looming, offer a study group or practice test session in which you can provide one-on-one assistance. Be sure to offer a break midway through the session with snacks and beverages. After the tests are over, turn these participants into regular customers by offering an ongoing study group, so they don't fall behind before the next big test.

▸ Conversation groups

If you have mastered a second language — or if English is your second language — host a night for others to practice their skills. This can be informal and held almost anywhere. It's best to have a small group and a few topics in mind for discussion. Your students will expect you to keep the conversation rolling and will want you to offer suggestions for improvement.

Have a few books on hand to reference and demonstrate proper spelling or conjugation. Talk with local travel agents to set up practice nights for their groups going to foreign countries — especially effective if you know Spanish, French, or Italian.

‣ Mini-camps

As with the sports or academic camps, parents look for children's day activities during school breaks — either to help students struggling with the subject or just for something to keep them occupied. Many parents send their children to "language immersion" camps where the kids can speak only the language being taught. You can offer this same type of experience in your own backyard. Team up with a few friends who also speak the language and build a camp around a few of the cultural experiences — give the kids crafts, snacks, and physical activity all while they are learning a language. Just be sure you have enough books, space, and patience to accommodate everyone.

‣ Transcription, translation, or interpretative services

If you have relatives nearby, you've probably already worked as an interpreter for their daily needs. From translating a letter to working as an intermediary with doctors or teachers, your second language skills can be invaluable to those needing help. Just be aware that these customers are relying on you and only you for accuracy and attention — there is little margin for error. *Check Appendix B for website postings of these types of jobs.*

Job Category: Sewing, Knitting, Crocheting, and Handiwork

When your grandparents were in school, sewing lessons were part of every girl's education. Obviously, things have changed drastically since then, and sewing is barely covered in home economics class. Even many adults your parents' age have limited sewing skills but still need alterations, mending, or big sewing projects completed. From hemming slacks to sewing Halloween costumes to creating custom drapery, if you know your way around a sewing machine or other handiwork, you can make money from these skills.

TIP!

Sewing is not limited to girls. If you have the skill and talent, put it to good use even if it is not considered a traditional man's job.

Potential hourly price range: You can expect to charge about $10 per hour for basic alterations, $15 to $20 per hour for sewing from patterns, $25+ per hour for original or large-scale creations. *Chapter 7 will cover how to create and sell your own handmade products; this section will focus on sewing for hire.*

Equipment or supplies needed: If you're working from your own home, you'll need the equipment and supplies required for your task, such as a sewing machine, thread, snaps and buttons, patterns, and so on. If you're working in your client's home, you can expect them to provide most of this equipment. It's nice to work with your own sewing machine, however, because you will know how to operate it.

Costs: Low if working off site, high if using your own equipment

Logistical considerations: Transportation to your client or a space to meet with them for fittings and consultations. You'll also need space to store your sewing while it is in progress. You might need to buy material and supplies up front before you are paid for the finished piece — consider asking for a partial payment before starting work so you have the funds to buy material.

Permits/licenses needed: None

Skills and education needed: You will need advanced knowledge of the type of handiwork you're doing. You can advance your skills through local sewing groups, community education offices, or by finding an experienced mentor.

Fits with these interests and attributes: Problem-solving skills, good attention to detail, like to help others, ability to meet deadlines, independent work-style

Your customer's profile:

Personal: The majority of your customers will be adults looking for help with alterations or big sewing projects such as holiday decorations or costume making. You can also find customers by setting up classes to teach sewing skills.

Business: Few standard businesses hire out sewing. However, you can find work by sewing holiday decorations such as Christmas window displays or offering your alteration services to upscale clothing stores to help fill in during busy seasons.

References needed: Yes, but minimal — your previous work will show your skills.

Seasonality: Any time of the year but might peak in the months before big holidays or event seasons

Safety issues: Personal safety issues related to working with strangers or sharp equipment such as sewing needles. Fittings can be awkward as you will be working closely with people in various states of undress, and you might have to work with finicky customers. You will also have to be careful not to damage your customer's irreplaceable clothing or expensive material.

Marketing ideas and how to reach your potential customers: Talk with your local dry cleaner — they are sometimes looking for extra help with mending and alterations. Spread the word to other parents that you can help with any small or large sewing job they need help with. Post a flier on local bulletin boards and at fabric stores. Take pictures of all your creations, and save in a portfolio you can show to potential customers.

Build in special offers and package deals or create group sessions: Provide your customers with a money-back guarantee in which you promise to make the piece to their satisfaction or they don't have to pay. Always offer a little bit of extra service — for example, if you're hired to alter a piece, take time to secure all the buttons. Offer your customers a discount for repeat business or for multiple items. If you're teaching, create a special holiday class from which your customers will take home a finished piece for their table.

Break it down and make it your own

‣ Personal tailor

The sky is the limit here, but you don't have to take on large-scale wardrobe projects to make money as a tailor. This is another area where breaking a job down into small, basic tasks can net you a big payday. Consider simple tasks such as sewing on buttons or replacing lost buttons, hemming new pieces, or shortening pants to be used as hand-me-downs. You can be assured that everyone has a basketful of mending they've been meaning to get to — this is one of the jobs you can take over. If you are ambitious, you can also take on jobs in which you sew complete outfits or special occasion pieces for people, such as a baptismal gown.

‣ Home décor sewing

With the popularity of do-it-yourself decorating, many homeowners are taking on these jobs but do not have the skills to finish their designs with fabric. They would love custom pieces made to match their décor but cannot afford the price of hiring a professional. With a simple consultation and your customer's fabric, you can easily create pillows, curtains, wall hangings, or table linens to suit their designs. You can also make one-of-a-kind pieces from handiwork such as crocheting, cross-stitching, quilting, and more.

> ## TIP!
>
> Do not forget all the special décor needed for the holidays — from bunting for the Fourth of July to place mats for Easter, people love to spruce up their homes with special, handmade items.

▸ Costume creation

Every Halloween, moms around the nation scramble for that perfect costume for their kids. You can be their hero by stepping in to do the sewing. This also can be fun for you as you help an entire family suit up for the holidays. Tailors also are called upon for stage productions to create costumes and set design — check with your local theater, and offer your services as part-time help. Also, if you live near a Renaissance Festival or other similar community event, you might find sewing jobs during these busy times.

▸ Restoration

Many families have special afghans, scarves, or treasured pieces handed down from previous generations that could use a little repair. If you know how to knit, crochet, or do needlepoint, you can offer a fix-it service to these people to help preserve their treasures. Make sure you can cope with the stress, though, of handling these one-of-a-kind and delicate pieces.

▸ Classes or mini-camps

Interest is growing among adults and older children in learning sewing and handiwork skills. Knitting has become especially popular and is quite easy to teach — you need minimal equipment or space, and your students will see nearly immediate rewards. You can easily put together a class to teach the basics or offer to help skilled sewers advance their skills. You could also offer a short half-day camp during school breaks for kids to drop in for a lesson. Just make sure you have enough patience, space, and supplies to accommodate your group.

Job Category: Mechanical Repair and Maintenance Service

Do you love tinkering in the garage, working on engines, or repairing mechanical parts? From replacing bike chains to getting the snow blower running, if you're mechanically inclined and know what you're doing, you can find steady work in your own neighborhood.

Potential hourly price range: You can expect to charge about $10 to $15 per hour. On-call and emergency services can be billed at $15 to $20 per hour.

Equipment or supplies needed: You'll need a good set of tools and spare parts related to the type of work you are doing. You'll also need access to manuals of the pieces you're repairing — most of these can be found online, so you'll probably need a laptop computer with Internet access. You can find some of these manuals at your library, or ask your customer to bring along the manual that came with the equipment.

Costs: High if you need to buy a lot of specialized tools, but these tools will last for a long time and are only a one-time, up-front cost.

Logistical considerations: You'll need a space to work on the repair or transportation of you and your tools to your customer's site. You'll also need a well-stocked collection of repair supplies or handy access to a store that sells what you need.

Permits/licenses needed: None

Skills and education needed: Depending on the type of work you're doing, you might need specialized technical know-how, but you can probably gather enough work using what you already know.

Fits with these interests and attributes: Problem-solving skills and good diagnostic abilities, good attention to detail, like to help others, independent work-style

Your customer's profile:

Personal: Your customer is anyone with a piece of equipment you know how to fix. Things with small engines such as lawn mowers, weed trimmers, and snow blowers are notorious for breaking down — if you can repair these engines you will be the neighborhood go-to guy. Your fellow bike or skateboard fans are also a good source of income if you can fix their equipment for them. Just don't start charging your friends and neighbors for work you usually would do free.

Business: Small, local businesses often have equipment repair needs, but the owners don't have the time or expertise to handle the repairs. You can be the person they call when something breaks down or for regular maintenance jobs. You can also offer your services to repair shops to help during their busy seasons. Working with established mechanics is a great way to build your own skills while you get paid.

References needed: Yes, but minimal — your work will prove your value.

Seasonality: Any time of the year but might peak with the change of seasons, such as mower repairs in the spring or fall

Safety issues: Personal safety issues related to working alone, with strangers, or with potentially dangerous mechanical equipment and tools. Your customer's personal safety and belongings can be put at risk if you do the repair improperly — such as a bike crash if you don't secure the chain correctly.

Marketing ideas and how to reach your potential customers: Word-of-mouth in your neighborhood will help you find customers. Post a flier at your local hardware store, and talk with the clerks to let them know you do engine or equipment repairs.

Build in special offers and package deals or create group sessions: This is a good area to use the bundling idea discussed earlier — if you're hired to fix a lawn mower, offer to do regular maintenance on your customer's other equipment. Remind them that maintaining their tools is usually more cost-effective than repairing them. Always offer extra services — if you're doing lawn-mower engine maintenance, offer to sharpen the blades as well.

Break it down and make it your own

Anything with moving parts, an engine, a cutting blade, or infrequent use needs maintenance and repair. You can focus on one specific area or expand your offering to cover just about anything. Make sure to only take on projects you're confident you can complete. Don't be afraid to ask for help from a more experienced mechanic if you run into trouble. Be sure you have enough time to finish the project because your customer is depending on that piece of equipment. Most of these tools also need special care at the beginning and end of each season. Offer a winterizing/dewinterizing service in which you clean the equipment, repair parts that have broken, sharpen blades, or put the piece away so it will work well in the next season. Here are just a few areas that fit well with part-time repair or maintenance work:

- Lawnmower — push or rider
- Weed whippers
- Leaf blowers or hedge trimmers
- Blade sharpening of garden tools and shovels
- Snow blowers
- Chain saws — motor repair or blade sharpening
- Small engines such as boat motors, kid's ATVs, or dirt bikes
- Large engines such as motorcycles, autos, inboard boat motors, snowmobiles
- Bicycle, scooter, or skateboard repair

Job Category: Carpentry or Handyman Service

Every homeowner has a to-do list filled with carpentry jobs of all sizes. Whether it's hanging a few shelves or remodeling an entire room, if you have carpentry skills or fix-it experience you can find tons of part-time, well-paying work. You don't have to be a licensed, bonded carpenter to fill your schedule with jobs — this is another area in which you can break jobs down into small pieces and still find plenty of opportunities.

TIP!

You don't have to be a "man" to be a handyman. Women are just as suited to fix-it work. If you have the skills, you can have the job.

Potential hourly price range: You can expect to charge approximately $10 to $15 per hour. More advanced carpentry projects can be billed at $15 to $20 per hour.

Equipment or supplies needed: It's best to start out with a basic tool box or belt with a heavy hammer, screwdrivers, tape measure, a level, and a stepladder. You can eventually upgrade to fancier tools, such as a cordless drill, but these are not necessary to find work. You'll also need sturdy work shoes, eye and ear protection, and clothes that can get dirty. Depending on the specific work you're doing, you might need more specialized equipment, such as tiling or drywalling tools.

Costs: High if you need to buy a lot of specialized tools — but these tools will last a long time and are only a one-time, up-front cost.

Logistical considerations: You'll need a space to work on your projects or a way to transport yourself and your tools to your customer's site. You'll also need a well-stocked collection of basic supplies such as nails or glue — or ready access to a store that sells what you need.

Permits/licenses needed: You don't need a license to do carpentry. However, some of the tasks you run across during construction must be completed or supervised by a licensed professional — these include jobs such as electrical, plumbing, or cement work. Most home projects do require a permit from local authorities, and you can expect the homeowner to handle acquiring the permit. The permit will list the jobs and stages that need inspection, and these are the tasks typically handled by a licensed professional. If you're taking on a large, permitted job, be sure to follow the inspection steps listed on the permit, or you might have to remove finished work for the inspector's visit.

Skills and education needed: Depending on the type of work you're doing, you might need specialized technical know-how, but you can probably gather enough work using what you already know.

Fits with these interests and attributes: Problem-solving skills and good attention to detail, independent work-style. But also must be able to follow instructions and have the ability to meet deadlines and complete a task

Your customer's profile:

Personal: Your customer is any homeowner with a small home repair need, fix-it job, or remodeling project. People getting ready for big events such as graduation are always looking to spruce up their homes and would love a helper for the day. Many older people can no longer handle the physical tasks needed to keep up with home repairs — even simple things like climbing a ladder to hang a picture or fixing a loose hand rail are jobs they're willing to hire out. Homeowners with busy lives also need help with home repairs and often will hire you to work alongside them to get the chores done. This is a great way for you to learn and build your skill level so you can eventually do these jobs on your own.

Business: Small, local businesses often have repair needs in their stores, but the owners don't have the time or expertise to handle them. You can be the person they call when something needs fixing. You can also look for work with professional carpenters to fill in as part-time help for big jobs or when they get busy and need an extra set of hands. Working with full-time carpenters is a great way to learn new skills and build up your experience.

References needed: Yes, but minimal — your work will prove your value.

Seasonality: Any time of the year but might peak during your area's construction season

Safety issues: Personal safety issues related to working alone, with strangers, or with potentially dangerous tools or on construction sites. Your customer's personal safety and belongings also can be put at risk if you do the repair improperly, such as a handrail coming loose if not adequately secured. Never cut corners or take on jobs you don't know how to complete.

Marketing ideas and how to reach your potential customers:
Word-of-mouth in your neighborhood will help you find customers.
Consider getting a few business cards to hand out when the opportunity
arises. Post a flier at your local hardware or building supply store, and talk
with the clerks to let them know you do small fix-it jobs. Take pictures of
your completed jobs and post to social networking sites — just be sure not
to post the personal information of your customers.

Build in special offers and package deals or create group sessions:
Offer a "helper for the day" special in which you discount your rate if they
hire you for a full day or long-term project. Set up return visits or give your
customers ideas for the next project you can help with. Offer a referral
discount if your customers share your name with others. Team up with a
friend and offer interior design services and the carpentry skills to complete
the designs.

Break it down and make it your own

▸ Light carpentry or construction

These are the quick jobs
that can be finished
in a couple of hours
and require just a few
tools: mirror or picture
hanging, small home
repairs such as touching
up paint scuffs or
tightening loose rails,
simple construction tasks

such as building a storage shelf. The list is endless and if you're willing to take instruction and have basic skills, you can find enough handyman jobs to fill a Saturday.

▸ Heavy construction or carpentry

These types of jobs require more skill, more tools, and are more physically demanding. It's possible, however, to find a lot of work in this area by working with a more established carpenter or an experienced homeowner who can guide you. Again, there's a broad range of tasks and each area has room for a beginner to help:

- Demolition and debris removal
- Framing and drywalling
- Tiling
- Trim or molding installation and other finish work
- Door hanging and fixture installation
- Painting
- Flooring installation or refinishing
- Cabinetry building and installation
- Siding or roofing removal or installation

▸ Furniture

Your carpentry skills can be put to use by making furniture to order based on your customer's designs or by assembling premade furniture sold in boxes at large department stores. This assembly requires a few tools, some time, and the patience to follow the instructions. A great market in furniture refinishing also exists — people have old pieces that need help or antiques they have been meaning to refinish. Often, these pieces only require a little elbow grease and a new coat of paint to bring them back to life. *Chapter 7 will cover how to build or refinish furniture to sell on your own.*

▸ Kid's classes

If you love kids, you could set up a short mini-camp or morning class to teach the little ones how to build something. Similar to the classes offered at Home Depot® or Michaels® crafts store, you have all the supplies and pieces cut out and ready to go when the kids arrive. During the session, you teach them how to assemble it, and they go home with a cute birdhouse or other little project they're proud to show off. Make sure you have enough room, supplies, and patience to accommodate everyone.

What Else Can You Do?

The world is full of unique hobbies, and these chapter listings are just a starting point for you. If your special interest or talent wasn't listed in this chapter, that doesn't mean you can't turn it into a job. If you're excited about it and know the topic well, you can most likely make money through others interested in the same thing. Be creative, take chances, and spread the word that you'd like to help. You never know who will call and where following your interests can lead you.

CHAPTER FIVE

Make Money Doing the Dirty Work

The carpets need to be vacuumed, lawns need to be mowed, and the windows need to be washed, but most adults are too busy to get everything done. So, who exactly is going to do all the chores? It could be you if you're willing to get your hands dirty to make some money. Most of these tasks fall squarely under the manual labor category of work, don't require a lot of advanced skills, and have been the realm of teens for generations. You do need some basic training, but if you handle these chores at home, you most likely know enough to find work.

Cleaning and yard work are definitely not the most glamorous jobs, but they are among the easiest jobs to find and keep. Most adults are happy to hire a teenager and hand over a time-consuming job such as weekly housecleaning or hedge trimming. For busy adults, your services will be money well spent if they help clear out their schedules a bit.

If you do a good job, your customers will also refer you to their friends, and you could end up with more work than you ever imagined. These jobs also transition well with you to college. No matter where you live, people always need help with cleaning and yard work. Gather references from every customer and keep them collected in one folder. When you start looking for work in a new place, these references will get you in the door.

Job Category: Indoor Cleaning

If your own household chores include dusting, vacuuming, and scrubbing floors, you have the necessary training to become a house cleaner. It's as simple as doing what you already do at home for someone else. Of course, you might have to take on whole houses, cleaning toilets, and perfectionist customers — but it still beats flipping burgers for minimum wage and still getting stuck cleaning the restaurant's bathrooms. Cleaning services don't have to include every cleaning chore possible, and you don't have to take on large tasks to earn cash. You can offer a limited, specialized service that only covers one cleaning need such as laundry, window cleaning, or office cleaning.

Potential hourly price range: You can expect to charge approximately $10 to $15 per hour — many cleaners charge by the job or by the level of cleaning needed. For instance, the fee for cleaning an entire house once a week can range from $50 to $150 depending on the square footage. Call around to local maid services to get an idea of the going rates, and set your fees at the lower end of this range.

Equipment or supplies needed: Most of your customers will provide the cleaning supplies and tools you need to do the job, but you might want to carry your own pair of rubber gloves. You'll also need clothes you don't mind getting dirty or splattered with cleaning solutions.

Costs: Zero to low if using your customer's supplies. High if providing your own equipment or supplies, but these costs can be added to your bill.

Logistical considerations: You'll need transportation to your work site.

Permits/licenses needed: None

Skills and education needed: You will need an understanding of basic cleaning techniques and the equipment needed for the task such as a washing machine or vacuum.

Fits with these interests and attributes: Problem-solving skills, good attention to detail, ability to take directions, independent work-style

Your customer's profile:

Personal: Anyone who needs help cleaning either because they are too busy to do it themselves or who are unable to do the cleaning due to illness or age, or people who just do not want to clean. You also might find one-time jobs for people hosting large events at their homes or those looking to clean up their houses before the holidays.

Business: Many small businesses will hire a reliable teenager to clean their offices or place of business, but you most likely will have to work after hours. You also can find temporary work as a fill-in for established cleaning companies who get too busy to handle all of their workload.

References needed: Yes, but minimal — your work will prove your value.

Seasonality: Any time of the year, but might peak before the holidays and busy social events such as graduation or weddings

Safety issues: Personal safety issues related to working alone, with strangers, or with toxic cleaning solutions. There's also the risk of damage to your customer's home or belongings, which could be broken or damaged during the cleaning process. Many times, you'll be given the keys or left alone in the home, so it will be your responsibility to make sure everything is securely protected and locked up when you are done. Keep your client's information private, and don't tell your friends or social network where you'll be working.

Marketing ideas and how to reach your potential customers: Ask your grandparents and parents to tell their friends that you can help with their cleaning needs. Post a flier at local stores and spread the word through social network sites. Referrals are essential here, so ask your customers to tell their friends about you.

Build in special offers and package deals or create group sessions: Offer gift certificates and specials such as a "new baby" cleaning special. This makes a great baby shower gift friends can buy for the new mom. Team up with a handyman friend to offer a spring cleaning and maintenance service in which you do the heavy cleaning while he or she helps with the home repair chores people do once a year. Give your current customers a referral discount or bonus when their referrals lead to new jobs.

Break it down and make it your own

▸ Regular daily or weekly cleaning

Once-a-week cleaning or twice monthly cleaning is the most common cleaning service people are looking for. This job covers a thorough clean of everything — dusting, vacuuming, changing sheets, bathrooms, furniture, and floors — and your customers will expect you to do it all. You should be able to clean an entire home in one day, but you can easily team up with a friend to work together.

TIP!

If you run across a stubborn cleaning problem, check out Heloise®'s helpful household tips at **www.heloise.com** for guides to cleaning everything and to making your own cleaning solutions.

▸ Green cleaning

Appeal to the organic and environmentally conscious crowd by offering a cleaning service that is earth-friendly. Check at your local library or go online to research green cleaning methods. Many times all you need is vinegar and water for a sparkling shine — it will clean just about anything, it is safe for the environment and you, and it is cheaper than store-bought cleaning products.

▸ Seasonal or special occasion deep cleaning

Many people cannot afford to pay for a once-a-week cleaner, but they need help for those big yearly cleaning chores such as window washing, carpet cleaning, wall scrubbing, and so on. These tasks are especially needed when people are getting ready for home events such as graduation or holiday parties. Offer to work alongside your customer or provide a team to get these chores done in a day. This deep clean can also be offered to your existing customers for an extra fee.

▸ Office and corporate cleaning

Small businesses need cleaning, but many times the owners are too busy to handle it. From front window washing to back room dusting to desktop cleaning, you can step in and take on these jobs. Most small offices such as insurance agents, car dealers, or your local library always need someone to come in and empty wastebaskets, dust shelves, and vacuum. Just remember that you'll most likely be working after hours when the offices are empty, and you'll have to take extra care in protecting confidential business information present in these offices.

▸ Laundry assistance

This is a specialized area of cleaning, but if you have the skill or desire to handle — or at least a tolerance for handling — other people's dirty laundry, you can make good money. Offer your customers specific services such as ironing or delicate clothing cleaning. Older people also might appreciate assistance with handling their laundry, especially if they live in multilevel homes or apartment buildings with remote laundry facilities. Helping out with laundry is a great add-on to a regular cleaning service and one for which you can charge extra.

Job Category: Outdoor Cleaning

As with indoor cleaning, everything that is outside needs to be cleaned regularly and especially as the seasons change. From grimy siding to messy garage shelves to patio fountains, homeowners have a lot of outside cleaning chores to get finished. Unlike indoor cleaning, however, some of these cleaning chores are essential maintenance tasks that must be done. An example of this is washing the siding every spring and fall. If this time-consuming job is not done and the soil is left too long on the home, the siding can become damaged or discolored permanently. Homeowners, though, have difficulty squeezing these chores into their schedules, and that is where you can help. Many of these outdoor chores do require a bit more training and mechanical aptitude.

Potential hourly price range: You can expect to charge approximately $10 per hour for basic home maintenance tasks such as washing siding and $15 to $20 for more advanced chores such as pond maintenance or seasonal winterizing.

Equipment or supplies needed: In most cases, you'll be able to use your customer's equipment. If you can afford it, though, buying your own equipment, such as a power washer, is a good investment because you won't have to worry about non-working equipment. You'll also need the necessary safety gear for your job such as good work shoes, clothing, work gloves, and ear and eye protection.

Costs: Low if using your customer's equipment, high if using your own equipment

Logistical considerations: If using your own equipment, you'll be expected to pay for gas to run it. You'll also need a place to store your gear and a way to transport it to your customer's location. Most equipment also needs periodic maintenance and winterizing, so you'll need the tools or the funds to perform these tasks.

Permits/licenses needed: None

Skills and education needed: You will need basic knowledge of the type of outdoor cleaning or chore you are doing. This information can be found online, in product manuals, or in home maintenance books available at your local library. You'll also need to know how to safely operate and handle the equipment or chemicals needed for your chores. As you become more proficient and knowledgeable, more advanced jobs will become available to you, and you'll be able to charge higher rates. You can, however, find plenty of work based on what you already know.

Fits with these interests and attributes: Problem-solving skills, good attention to detail, like to help others, independent work-style

Your customer's profile:

Personal: Every homeowner, especially those with busy schedules such as parents of young children or people who travel a lot for work. You can also find work with older people who can no longer handle the chores alone but still live in large homes. You also might find one-time jobs for people hosting large events at their homes or those looking to clean up their houses or yards before the holidays.

Business: Most businesses hire these chores out to professional maintenance companies, but you might be able to find temporary work as a fill-in for established cleaning companies who get too busy to handle all of their workload. If you live in an area with seasonal rentals, you might also find work helping out when it gets busy as the seasons end and begin.

References needed: Yes, but minimal — your work will prove your value.

Seasonality: Any time of the year, but work might peak at the change of the seasons

Safety issues: Personal safety issues related to working alone, with strangers, or with potentially dangerous equipment and toxic chemicals; damage to your customer's home or landscaping if the work is done improperly

Marketing ideas and how to reach your potential customers: Your best marketing tactic is to advertise your services as a "protection of investment" for your customers. For example, the cost to replace the siding on a home can be more than $15,000 — your minor fee of $50 to $100 for yearly washing potentially can save the homeowner thousands in costly repairs. Most homeowners are aware of these needs but run out of time to get it all done, and the chores are put off or forgotten. Spread the word throughout your neighborhood, and post fliers in local hardware or grocery stores. Consider getting T-shirts, hats, or business cards printed to advertise your services, and ask your clients for referrals.

Build in special offers and package deals or create group sessions: Team up with a friend to offer a full-service home and yard package. Your friend can handle the lawn work while you take care of the outdoor cleaning chores. Give your current customers a referral discount or bonus when their referrals lead to new jobs. Upsell to your existing customers by pointing out additional services you can take on.

Break it down and make it your own:

▸ Pond, fountain, or water feature cleanup and maintenance

Many homes now have outdoor water features, such as ponds or fountains, as part of the landscaping. Over time, these ponds can build up scum or debris that settles onto the water surface. Not only can this debris gum up the mechanics of the pumps, it can also be unsightly and cause algae to grow. Put together a twice-a-month service to come by and clean things out. In colder climates, the water and pumps need to be cleaned up before winter freezes and put back in place after spring thaws.

▸ Pool or hot tub maintenance or seasonal care

As with small water features, pools or hot tubs require regular maintenance and upkeep for the water to stay clean and the machinery to function properly. Unlike small ponds, though, keeping water quality at proper quality levels is essential to avoid health problems for users. Many homeowners, though, find the maintenance schedule to be too hard to keep up with, and this is where you can help. Just make sure you follow the manufacturer's recommendations and handle pool chemicals with extreme care.

▸ Garage or workshop cleaning

Most guys can tell you that keeping their garages and workshops clean is a never-ending task, but having a clean shop makes every home project easier. Put together a garage cleanup service in which you put in one or two hours every Saturday to help straighten and organize the workshop or garage space. You also can offer a deep clean in which you clean down to the walls and help throw out all the junk that's accumulated.

▸ Siding, patio, or deck pressure washing

As mentioned earlier, keeping the grime off the siding, deck, or patio is an important home maintenance chore that's often skipped by busy homeowners. If you have your own pressure washer, you can practically haul it from house to house and find work every Saturday. Just make sure you know how to adjust the pressure settings properly for the type of cleaning you're tackling because water pressure that is too high can damage the materials you're washing. Ask the homeowner to review the manual or go online for tips on the best settings and chemicals to use for each particular project.

▸ Window washing

Washing windows was touched on the Indoor Cleaning section, but it also falls under the Outdoor category. A thorough window washing includes removing the screens and scrubbing them down, washing all the grime out of the windowsills, and cleaning the outside portion of the windows. In older homes, this is a time-consuming and physically demanding task, as you need to remove the windows or screens from the outside, and you'll need to climb up and down a ladder. Most homeowners tackle this big job in the spring and fall — older people are your best bet for finding customers for window washing.

Job Category: Household Chores

In addition to cleaning, many people need help around the house or in running errands. Older people have trouble carrying things or climbing ladders to reach high places. Young parents are too busy to get everything done. Busy families with older kids spend their weekends running around to sports and other activities. You can step in to be that helper and tick off their to-do list items while they attend to more important things. By working alongside homeowners or older people to get their chores done, you'll gain some valuable life skills and experience.

Potential hourly price range: You can expect to charge approximately $10 per hour plus mileage if you're running errands.

VOCAB

Mileage refers to the costs accrued while operating a vehicle for work purposes, and the reimbursement covers everything from wear and tear on the vehicle to actual gas used. If you're charging mileage to your customer, discuss beforehand how they want you to calculate it. The simplest method is to charge a fixed rate per mile driven. The going tax rate as of 2012 is 55.5 cents per mile. You'll need to keep written records of your driving with details on where you drove and the work purpose of each trip.

Equipment or supplies needed: Your customers should have whatever you need to accomplish their chores, although your own car or bike will come in handy if you're running errands.

Costs: Zero unless using your own car

Logistical considerations: None

Permits/licenses needed: None unless you'll be driving your customer's car. In this instance, you'll need a driver's license and proper insurance coverage. Check with your parents and your customer to make sure you have the necessary policy to cover you while driving.

Skills and education needed: Depending on the type of work you're doing, you'll only need to know how to do everyday things such as changing light bulbs, carrying in groceries, and so on. In most cases, your customers will tell you what to do, and all you will need to do is follow their directions.

Fits with these interests and attributes: Problem-solving skills, good attention to detail, ability to follow directions, and independent work-style. You must have excellent communication and people skills to succeed at this job.

Your customer's profile:

Personal: All ages, renters and homeowners, and anybody who just needs occasional help around the house

Business: You might find some work for small business owners in running errands for their business or personal life. Professional organizers and moving companies also might give you temporary work to meet their overflow.

References needed: Yes, but minimal — your work will prove your value.

Seasonality: Any time of the year

Safety issues: Personal safety issues related to working alone, with strangers, or if doing physical labor. There's the potential of damage to your customer's belongings or home if you mishandle something or do the job improperly.

Marketing ideas and how to reach your potential customers: Word-of-mouth and social networking will get you plenty of work. Spread the word around your neighborhood and among your parents' and grandparents' friends. Post fliers in community centers or at senior citizen apartment complexes advertising your services. Remember that no job is too small. Once you get your foot in the door, you'll most likely get more work.

Build in special offers and package deals or create group sessions: Give a referral discount to your existing customers when they refer a friend that results in new work. Team up with friends to offer a full-service package that includes your assistance and their cleaning abilities. Offer specials built around special events or holidays unique to your community. For instance, make a Mother's or Father's Day package in which adults hire you to help their aging parents for a day.

Break it down and make it your own:

▶ Regular household helper

This job encompasses every little chore or errand that is required to run a home. From changing light bulbs or smoke detector batteries to carrying in and stashing groceries to carrying Christmas decorations down from the attic, you could help with hundreds of small tasks. Typically, you'll be hired on for a couple of hours, and your customer will give you multiple tasks to accomplish.

▸ Decluttering and organization service

Everyone has a closet, attic, or basement storage space that needs a good cleaning. In most homes, these spaces become the dumping grounds for old, worn-out, and seldom-used items. You can help by clearing out the old and organizing whatever is left in conveniently labeled and shelved boxes. Don't forget parents with preteens. They have toy rooms and garage shelves filled with stuff kids are no longer using. *Chapter 7 will cover selling these cast-offs on eBay or at garage sales.*

▸ Moving muscle

Whether your customer is redecorating the living room or packing up the whole house for a move, you can provide the muscle to get things moving. Many older people just need help to move things around for new arrangements. People who are packing up their homes can use the extra assistance to pack things and get the  boxes moved to a central location. Consider posting your flier at local truck rental companies offering assistance in packing and unpacking boxes or moving furniture.

Job Category: Outdoor Chores and Yard Work

In addition to regular cleaning, homeowners also need to deal with regular outside chores and yard work every week. From keeping the grass cut to raking leaves to shoveling snow, every season brings a new job with it. Even with adequate time to complete the job, many people don't want to spend their weekends on these chores or don't have the physical stamina to handle the work. It doesn't take a lot of experience, and if you've been doing these chores at home already, you're well qualified to do the work for others. You don't have to restrict yourself to grass cutting, and the options for outside garden work are limited only by your willingness to work.

Potential hourly price range: You can expect to charge approximately $10 per hour for basic lawn care such as mowing, watering, or raking. More skilled services such as tree trimming or landscape maintenance can be charged at $12 to $15 per hour.

Equipment or supplies needed: Your customer should have all the equipment you need. If you can afford it, though, buying the tools you'll be using is worth the investment because you won't have to worry about non-working equipment. You'll also need to have the necessary safety gear required for the job such as good work shoes, appropriate clothing, ear and eye protection, and sunscreen.

Costs: Low if using your customer's equipment, high if using your own equipment

Logistical considerations: If using your own equipment, you'll be expected to pay for gas to run it. You'll also need a place to store your tools and a way to transport them. Most equipment also needs periodic maintenance and winterizing, so you'll need the tools or the funds to perform these tasks.

Permits/licenses needed: None

Skills and education needed: Depending on the type of work you're doing, you might need specialized knowledge such as training in proper pruning methods or fertilizer application levels. This information can be found online or in any basic gardening book. For simple chores such as lawn mowing or leaf raking, you can probably gather enough work using what you already know. You'll also need to know how to safely operate and maintain the equipment you are using.

Fits with these interests and attributes: Good attention to detail, like to help others, independent work-style, ability to handle physical labor, ability or desire to work outside

Your customer's profile:

Personal: Anyone with a lawn, a sidewalk, potted plants, or a tree that drops its leaves. The best part about providing outside assistance is that most of these jobs need to be done on a regular basis, and your customers will need you to come back week after week. If you do a good job, you can count on a regular payday, and you won't have to go looking for new customers.

Business: Many small businesses also maintain landscaping or flower pots around their offices and will be happy to hire you to maintain these spaces for them. You also can find temporary seasonal overflow work from professional lawn care services or from businesses that maintain large outside spaces such as colleges or golf courses.

References needed: Yes, but minimal — your work will prove your value.

Seasonality: Depending on your climate and the type of work you're doing, this can be a year-round job.

Safety issues: You will be working with potentially dangerous tools, climbing ladders, moving heavy objects, handling toxic chemicals, or working in hot conditions. You, the people around you, or your customers' belongings also can be injured by rocks or sticks flying out of the mower. Talk with your parents or another adult about proper handling, and wear sunscreen, use protective gear, and bring a big jug of water with you. You'll also have personal safety issues related to working alone or with strangers.

Marketing ideas and how to reach your potential customers: Spreading the word through your parents' network of friends, talking with your neighbors, or posting a flier at local businesses will net you plenty of work. Many older people or busy families find it difficult to get the lawn work done, and these are great groups to look to. Remember that just one acquired job will mean regular weekly work, so be sure you don't take on too many jobs at first.

Build in special offers and package deals or create group sessions: Offer your customers as many extras as possible — just make sure to spell out the fee for each task so they don't think you're doing it all for one price. For example, if you're already mowing the lawn once a week, offer to do additional pruning, fertilizing, or watering once a month. Make sure your customer knows you can continue working as the seasons change; you can go from mowing to raking to shoveling to spring cleanup and have year-round work. You can also team up with friends who enjoy gardening to provide landscape design or garden planning services.

Break it down and make it your own:

▸ Regular or weekly chores

This covers it all from mowing the grass to keeping the driveway free of snow. Once you're hired, you'll be expected to show up when the work needs to be done. This means you might have lots of work for one week and not much the next. It also means you will have to arrange for substitute help if you are unavailable. Most homeowners are willing to work around your schedule as long as you let them know when you have a conflict. It is also important to thoroughly discuss the scope of work you're expected to accomplish for the price you are charging. For example, if you're mowing lawns, you can offer to remove the clippings as part of the base fee, but other trimming jobs will cost extra. You can offer whatever services you like for your price but make sure you remain competitive with others in your area.

▸ Advanced or heavy-duty chores

Mowing is just the beginning of the to-do list for those with big lawns, and you can make a lot of money by taking on these additional chores. The sky is the limit, and as you gain experience with specialty services, you can begin to charge more. Browse through a gardening book to get an idea of the type of work you can offer to homeowners, and pick one area you'd like to specialize in, such as garden tilling, pruning and tree trimming, patio block laying, or sidewalk edging. These chores aren't limited to summer and can include fall gutter cleanout, snow roof removal, or splitting and stacking firewood for the winter.

▶ Seasonal helper

If your schedule is too full to take on regular weekly work, you can also make money by helping out with the change of the seasons. Raking the leaves or cleaning up the lawn in the spring is a big job, and many homeowners will be happy to have a helper. People with big outside events such as graduation or summer parties often are looking for assistance in getting the lawn spruced up before these events.

▶ Vacationer's helper

People who take a week away in the summer or snowbirds that fly south for the winter still need the lawn mowed, the flowers watered, or the snow shoveled while they are away. People that keep vacation homes also need assistance keeping their yards spiffed up in between visits. Check with local rental agencies and realtors who often help arrange summer home care for their clients. Depending on where you live, you could find enough vacation helper's work to keep you busy all summer long.

Job Category: Automotive Care

Visit any car wash on a Saturday morning, and you'll see there are big bucks to be made in regular weekly car cleaning. Car owners can pay $50 or more per cleaning if they order the "complete car care" package from a professional detailer. You can easily provide the same services for a lot less money, and all it takes are a few simple tools and a bit of car-care knowledge. You don't need mechanical abilities, only a good eye for cleaning and the perseverance to crawl around and clean out every nook and cranny.

> ## TIP!
>
> Cleaning is not limited to cars — people with ATVs, snowmobiles, dirt bikes, or anything else that gets dirty need help with cleaning.

Potential hourly price range: You can expect to charge approximately $10 per hour or $20 to $40 per car depending on the scope of service.

Equipment or supplies needed: You'll be able to use your customers' equipment or take the car to a local car wash for most of the cleaning. Your job will be easier, though, if you assemble your own car-care kit and take it with you from job to job. The basic kit should include car cleaning solutions, rags, sponges, and a small handheld vacuum. You'll have to make a small investment in supplies, but then you won't need to spend your work time looking for cleaners or dealing with the subpar equipment found at many small car washes.

Costs: Low if using your customers' equipment, medium if using your own equipment

Logistical considerations: You'll need transportation of yourself and your supplies to your customer's home.

Permits/licenses needed: None unless you'll be driving your customers' cars. In this instance, you'll need a driver's license and proper insurance coverage. Check with your parents and your customer to make sure you have the necessary policy to cover you while driving.

Skills and education needed: You'll need to know how to clean many different types of vehicles. Both the interior and exterior of vehicles require unique cleaning methods and specialized cleaning products. These specifications are listed in the car's manual or can be found online. Be sure to ask the car owner for information or recommendations before you start working.

Fits with these interests and attributes: Problem-solving skills, good attention to detail, like to help others, independent work-style

Your customer's profile:

Personal: Car care is similar to housecleaning and yard work. Some people are meticulous about it, and others only clean their cars when it's absolutely necessary. Your customers can be any of these people, but you'll probably get the most work from those who like a weekly cleaning but don't want to pay the big bucks charged by professional services. You can also beat out the competition by coming to your customer's home, so they can avoid waiting in line at the car wash.

Business: Businesses that keep a fleet of work vehicles always can use help with the cleaning needs. As with personal customers, many business owners are picky about their vehicles but will be happy to hire someone who knows what they are doing.

References needed: Yes, but minimal — your work will prove your value.

Seasonality: Any time of the year, but it might peak in the spring or winter when cars get dirty from sloppy road conditions.

Safety issues: You will have personal safety issues related to working alone or with strangers. You also will be dealing with expensive vehicles and have the potential risk of damage to the paint, upholstery, or components if the cleaning is done improperly.

Marketing ideas and how to reach your potential customers: Social networking is a great way to find potential customers. Gather referrals from current customers, and post them for others to read. Take a before and after picture of a car you have cleaned, and post that online. Put up fliers at local businesses and especially on bulletin boards at car washes, auto parts stores, or hardware stores. Get to know the car enthusiasts in your area, and ask if they need help maintaining their vehicles.

Build in special offers and package deals or create group sessions: Offer your customers as many perks as possible. Even a free air freshener when you are finished will keep them coming back. Give referral discounts whenever customers send you new business. Offer a prom cleanup or back-from-vacation package in which you get the car ready for the special occasion or clean it out after a family's car trip. Make your own gift certificates so people can buy your car cleaning services as presents to give for the holidays or birthdays.

Break it down and make it your own:

▶ Regular washes and detailing

As with the maintenance chores listed in the previous sections, car cleaning is a job that most people try to accomplish every week or so. It's one of the jobs that takes time and often is rushed over or ignored altogether, when life gets busy. You can be the hero and step in to provide this necessity. Visit any local car care center and review their offerings — develop your service to match this and keep your prices low, and you'll find lots of work. Remember that once you're hired, you'll be expected to show up on a regular basis, so be sure to not take on more than you can handle.

▶ Heavy-duty cleanup

This can range from cleaning dirty work trucks to getting a used car cleaned up and ready to sell. Most people only hire a heavy-duty cleaner every few months, so this type of service will fit well with your schedule if you are too busy to take on regular weekly work. If you're handy, you can also help with minor interior repairs to dashboards, upholstery, or larger fixes like outside paint touch-ups.

▶ Car dealer's helper

The next time you drive by your local car dealership, count how many cars are parked in their lot. Every one of those cars needs to be kept clean and shiny, and the windows need to be scraped each time it snows. This is the perfect job for a teenager, but you'll have to be on call for the nights when the snow falls. Working in this capacity for a car dealer is also a great way to gain referrals and get your foot in the door for further car maintenance work.

Job Category: Farm or Ranch Hand

Farmers' or ranchers' lists of chores never end, and many of the jobs are tedious and time-consuming. If you are comfortable around animals or large machinery and can handle putting in a good day's work, you can make a lot of money helping on the farm. You'll also gain valuable skills as you work alongside the farmer, and you probably even will be fed a good meal at the end of the day. If you already live on a farm or have access to growing space, you can also raise your own produce, plants, or animals to sell. *This subject will be covered in Chapter 7.*

Potential hourly price range: You can expect to charge approximately $10 per hour for basic farm work, $15 to $20 per hour for more advanced animal care or machinery operation.

Equipment or supplies needed: The equipment should be provided by the farmer; however, come to work dressed appropriately with work boots and gloves, a brimmed hat, and your own water jug.

Costs: Zero to low

Logistical considerations: You'll need reliable transportation to rural locations, and you'll probably need to begin work in the early morning hours.

Permits/licenses needed: None unless operating machinery or vehicles, in which case you'll need the proper licenses and insurance coverage. Large machinery, such as tractors, requires a class of license more advanced than a regular driver's license.

Skills and education needed: If you're hired to do basic menial labor such as baling hay, you'll only need the muscles to throw heavy bales on a wagon. If you're hired to work closely with animals, you'll need the necessary background to keep yourself and the animals out of harm's way. Most ranchers are willing to help you, though, and are always happy to work with people who are eager to learn.

Fits with these interests and attributes: Problem-solving skills, good attention to detail, good physical condition, like to work with animals and in the outdoors, independent work-style

Your customer's profile:

Personal: Most of your customers will be farm and ranching businesses. If you have a lot of farming experience, you might find personal customers looking for help in setting up their own small farming operations.

Business: Most farms and ranches keep a few farmhands on as permanent employees, but they can always use help during the busy spring planting, fall harvesting, or animal handling times. Jobs will vary widely according to your area and expertise and could include hay baling, milking, equipment maintenance, or barn repairs.

References needed: Yes, but minimal — your work will prove your value.

Seasonality: Any time of the year but might peak during the fall and spring

Safety issues: Farm work is considered one of our nation's most hazardous professions and is especially dangerous for teens. The potential for problems exists everywhere on a farm from slips and falls to run-ins with unruly animals to equipment mishaps. It is critically important when working on a farm to follow safety rules to the letter, always work with someone else nearby, and never operate machinery beyond your capability.

Sidebar

Because of the inherent danger, the Department of Labor has set specific rules for teens and farm work. For these rules and great safety tips, visit their website at **www.youthrules.dol.gov** and click on the "teen" link.

Marketing ideas and how to reach your potential customers: You can connect with potential customers by visiting your local farmers market and talking with the producers there. Spread the word through your parents' network of friends or stop by farms where you would like to work. If you have friends who live on farms, let them know you are looking for work.

Build in special offers and package deals or create group sessions: Team up with a few friends, so you can offer a group to get the work done. This comes in especially handy when farmers are looking for crews to bring in crops or handle overflow such as when they get in new animal stock.

Break it down and make it your own:

▸ Regular or daily chores

The work never ends on a farm, especially with animals around. If you have experience handling farm animals, you can find steady work as a fill-in farm hand. From milking cows to gathering eggs to keeping everybody fed and watered, the chores happen every day like clockwork. Most farms do have regular employees to handle these chores, but they can often use someone to fill in for vacation or sick day coverage.

▸ Seasonal work

On top of the regular chores, each season brings a new crop of work to the farmer. Even if the farm has regular employees, they are working full time to get the daily work done. You can help fill in with the jobs that pop up such as mending fences, picking rocks, fixing up barns or machinery, baling hay, and so on. These type of jobs are physically demanding and do require some mechanical or farming expertise.

▸ Advanced animal care

If you're experienced with specific animal care such as grooming or breaking horses, raising chickens, or shearing sheep, you can find specialty work with these animals. You'll have to prove yourself to get hired. If you have 4-H or county fair ribbons or other experience, let the farmer know. Offer to work for a few hours free to prove you know what you are doing. You also can charge more per hour if you have advanced animal knowledge.

CASE STUDY: ON THE JOB WITH JONATHAN DEAN MARTIN KRALING

Occupation: Farming
Age: Started his business
around age 13

Jonathan Kraling in front of his farm. Photo courtesy of Jonathan Kraling.

Like most farm kids, I have been doing farm work my whole life, and my dad and grandpa taught me everything I know. Also, like many farm kids, I started young by raising animals on my own and raised my first steer together with my sister. After we sold it, we split the cash, and I put my portion in the bank. I continued to save my money through these types of sales until I eventually could buy my own cattle. I start with calves and raise them until they can be sold at market. Raising beef cows is more than just putting them out to pasture and waiting for them to get fat. This job involves a lot of up-front expenses and physically demanding, time-consuming chores including baling hay, buying feed, hauling manure, treating sick animals, and taking care of anything else the cattle need to grow.

Luckily, my dad lets me use his equipment and barns to take care of my cattle. I pitch in by helping out with all of the farm's chores and pay for all the supplies and feed needed for my share of the cattle. I sell my cattle at livestock auctions but also through word-of-mouth to people looking to buy beef. Farming is hard work, and I put in a lot of hours, but I think I've made more money than most of my non-farming friends. With this money, I bought my own truck and my own snowmobile, and I put money back into my business.

Working for myself but alongside my dad is a great experience, and I've learned a lot. I'm also proud of myself because I'm carrying on the family traditions and feel like I'm following in my grandpa's footsteps. This achievement is definitely worth more to me than money.

Words of Wisdom: Save your money; it will help you in the end. Also, my dad has always said, "Work hard when you're young and play later." Now that I'm older, I agree with him and know that hard work does pay off.

CHAPTER SIX

Make Money by Helping Out

If you've skimmed through the last few chapters, you're probably starting to think that adults spend all their time just trying to cross things off their to-do lists. In some ways, you're right. Keep in mind, though, that one of the reasons adults hold down professional jobs is so they can afford a certain standard of living. This standard of living often includes hiring someone to take care of the kids once in awhile, set the tables for big parties, or walk the dog during family vacations. Adults also have the advantage of making a good salary, and often the decision to hire someone like you comes down to simple financial common sense. For instance, if Mrs. Smith works at her job making $75 per hour, it makes more sense to pay someone $10 to run errands than to take an hour off work to do it herself. That is where you can step in and make that $10 per hour, which is still good money for a teenager.

Helping others falls into two broad categories: You work as a sort of personal assistant or you take on the responsibility of caring for a child, older person, or pet. Teenagers, of course, have been hired as babysitters for many generations, and this standard job will be covered in the following sections. Personal care, though, can go way beyond a Friday night babysitting gig and can cover everything from checking in on an elderly neighbor to walking the dog after school. You will, however, be responsible for their well-being, and sometimes your "customer" can be quite challenging. Just make sure you're capable of handling this responsibility, and don't take on more than you're comfortable with. Before taking on the care of another person or pet, consider meeting with your potential client to make sure you're compatible and will get along.

Job Category: Holiday, Party, or Special Occasion Helper

Previous chapters have covered various ways to make money from holiday events or special occasions such as graduation, but beyond singing, cooking, and cleaning, some people just need help pulling it all together. From wrapping presents to addressing Christmas cards to setting up tables, offer your assistance, and you'll find lots of work. Just remember that the holiday season might be a busy time for you,  too, so don't take on so much work that you end up missing your own celebrations. You can also run the risk of "holiday overload," and by the time the big day rolls around, you'll be tapped out of holiday spirit.

Potential hourly price range: You can expect to charge approximately $10 to $15 per hour. If using your own vehicle to run errands, you can charge mileage in addition to your hourly rate.

Equipment or supplies needed: You should be able to use your customer's supplies and equipment for whatever job you're doing. If you prefer a certain type of tool for the job, such as your favorite scissors, feel free to bring your own supplies when you come to work. If you're planning to work at the actual event, you'll need appropriate attire. Be sure to ask your clients what type of clothing they'd like you to wear.

Costs: Zero to low

Logistical considerations: You'll need transportation to your customer's home and might need your own transportation for running errands. If you're helping with decorating, you'll have to climb up a ladder and potentially work outside in inclement weather. If you're working with hired help or rental companies, you'll want a cell phone, so you can make calls from the event venue.

Permits/licenses needed: None unless you will be driving your customers' cars. In that instance, you'll need a driver's license and proper insurance coverage. Check with your parents and your customer to make sure you have the necessary policy to cover you while driving someone else's vehicle.

Skills and education needed: No special skills are needed to be a holiday helper, just the ability to understand and follow directions given to you by your client.

Fits with these interests and attributes: Good attention to detail, like to help others, ability to follow directions and work without supervision, creative thinker, independent and organized work-style

Your customer's profile:

Personal: Anyone getting ready for a holiday or special occasion. From Halloween to retirement parties to bar mitzvahs, if the event needs decorations, food, presents, invitations, or errand running, you can find work.

Business: Most businesses hire professionals to plan and execute their parties. However, if you've worked for a personal client, you might be able to gain a referral to his or her place of business. This referral could lead to small, odd jobs related to their events. You might also find overflow work from party planners or local decorators.

TIP!

Remember to develop your work in small chunks. You don't have to throw an entire party for your customer. Just taking over a small job such as hand delivering invites or addressing thank-yous is enough help for most people.

References needed: Yes, but minimal — your work will prove your value.

Seasonality: Any time of the year but will peak during the events and holidays common to your community. Many people start their holiday planning and errands months in advance; so don't wait until the last minute to start looking for work.

Safety issues: Personal safety issues related to working alone, with strangers, or if carrying boxes or climbing ladders. You'll also be partly responsible for the success or failure of the events, which often are once-in-a-lifetime and cannot be recreated if something goes wrong.

Marketing ideas and how to reach your potential customers: Referrals and word-of-mouth are the best way to find new customers. Ask your clients for a referral or repeat business. Take lots of pictures of the work you've done, or keep a record of each event and post these details to social network sites. Use these picture and records to create a mini-portfolio to show to prospective clients. Be sure to spread the word among your parents' and grandparents' friends and your neighbors.

Build in special offers and package deals or create group sessions: Once you have worked an event for someone, offer them ideas for how you can help out the next time. For example, if you've decorated someone's yard for Halloween, offer to come back and change everything out for the next holiday. Team up with a few friends to offer a crew to get bigger jobs done. Many people develop their work offerings based on the size of the available workforce. If you have more people, you'll probably gain more work.

Break it down and make it your own:

▸ Party planner or party assistant

Many people love to throw theme parties, but they don't know where to start. If you have a knack for organization and coming up with creative ideas, you can find work as a party planner. Theme parties can be thrown for just about any special occasion: baby or bridal showers, Mardi Gras, kids' or adults' birthdays, or just for the fun of it. Look online or check at your library, and you'll find hundreds of party books to get your ideas flowing. Even if you aren't creating the theme, you can help track down decorations, special food, or run errands for the hostess.

▸ Entertainment coordinator

The best parties always have a showstopper or a special touch that everyone leaves talking about. It might be a DJ with great tracks, pony rides for the kids, a magician or hypnotist to keep everyone mesmerized, or a collection of bouncy houses for the rambunctious — or maybe it's a combination of all these things. You can offer the party host assistance in tracking down entertainers, keeping tabs on them so they show up on time, and making sure all their equipment is properly set up and taken down. If you or your friends have special talents such as making balloon animals or face painting, you can also offer these entertainment services out for hire.

CASE STUDY: ON THE JOB WITH AVERY FRIX

Occupation: Owner and operator, Oxford Productions
Age: Started his business at age 15
avery-frix@oxfordmuskogee.com
www.oxfordmuskogee.com

Avery Frix at work at his sound board.

I began my own business in ninth grade by pursuing something I loved to do — sound and light production for theaters and public events. I'd been involved in the theater most of my school years, so I decided to turn my passion into a way to make money. At first, I bought minimal equipment, and then as I met people at events, I found they were willing to loan me the extra equipment I needed. As I made more money, I put it back into my business to purchase additional pieces of gear.

Networking and word-of-mouth was and continues to be an essential part of my business. I get all of my new business through my friends, family, and people I meet at the events I'm working. I try to be as personable as possible and use these connections to promote my company and secure new gigs. Through my networking at these events, I also find people I can hire as temporary workers either as performers or as crew to set up or tear down. Of course, the line between being a friend and being a boss can become blurred, so I've had to learn to manage these relationships and still get the job done.

My success and reinvestment has allowed me to expand my business into video production, DJ services, and event planning. I do work a lot and have found that my job requires me to put in long hours, especially on weekends. I've also learned that I won't be getting a steady paycheck, and instead, my money will come in spurts, such as when I'm paid for one event. Even with these drawbacks, I'm sure I'm making more money than my peers are working at regular jobs. Plus, I get to do something I love and enjoy.

Words of Wisdom: Do what you love, and take the advice of those you trust.

▸ Party waiter or busboy

For large events with sit-down meals, hostesses love to have help getting the meal out to the guests and clearing up tables after dinner. Many catering companies provide their own wait staff, but if the hostess is preparing the food herself, she will need help waiting tables. Just make sure you don't serve alcohol if you are underage — both you and the party host could get in trouble.

▸ Setup, cleanup, and takedown helper

Once the theme is chosen, someone needs to handle the logistics of the event. From renting and setting up chairs and tables to removing the streamers when it is all over, you can step in and make these jobs go smoothly. You'll have to work closely with the hostess to select the right supplies, and you'll need a crew to help move and set things up. You'll have a short amount of time to get the set up in place, so be sure you have enough helpers.

▸ Yard and home decorator

Getting lights, garlands, trees, and decorations set up takes a lot of physical labor. For holiday decorating, things usually need to be hauled from storage and unpacked. Outside lights require a few trips up and down the ladder. Party decorations also need some high-reaching help, and older people sometimes cannot handle this amount of work. You can find preseason and postseason work just from hauling and packing up the decorations everyone has stored in their attics and basements.

▸ Shopping and wrapping service

Believe it or not, some people don't like shopping. As a teenager, that is probably hard to fathom, but when the holidays roll around, that list of presents to buy gets pretty long. You can become someone's personal shopper. That is right. Getting paid to shop with someone else's money. You also can assist by bringing those presents home and getting them wrapped and stashed away until the big day arrives.

Job Category: Realtor's or Landlord's Helper

Most real estate agents are self-employed or work for small agencies with not a lot of extra helpers. Many times, though, these realtors have to handle a wide range of tasks that include everything from putting up open house signs to keeping lawns mowed to making sure unoccupied houses are cleaned and ready for a showing. The same situation exists for those renting their houses to vacationers or on a more permanent basis. Cleaning, yard work, and maintenance need to be done on these houses just as much as on regular houses, but these people don't have the extra staff to get it all done. You can be that fill-in person to help when things get busy.

Potential hourly price range: You can expect to charge approximately $10 per hour. On-call services can be billed at $15 to $20 per hour.

Equipment or supplies needed: Depending on the type of work you're doing, you might need a small tool kit or basic cleaning supplies, as you won't be able to find these at unoccupied homes.

Costs: Low to medium depending on the equipment you buy

Logistical considerations: You'll need your own transportation, as you'll be traveling to many different locations. You'll also need a map, a GPS, or a good understanding of locations in your community. You might have to work weekends or evenings.

Permits/licenses needed: You'll need a driver's license and proper car insurance. If you're driving your customers' cars, make sure you have the necessary insurance policy to cover you while driving someone else's vehicle.

Skills and education needed: The skills needed to perform this job will vary with the work. Generally, basic understanding of cleaning, maintenance, or yard work will be enough to get by.

Fits with these interests and attributes: Ability to follow directions and adapt to changing situations, problem-solving skills, good attention to detail, like to help others, good communication and people skills

Your customer's profile:

Personal: Most of your customers will be business-oriented, although you can find work with some people who are renting out only one or two properties out of necessity, such as a summer cabin or personal residence.

Business: Small realtors and small rental offices that have many properties to maintain and manage

References needed: Yes, but minimal — your work will prove your value.

Seasonality: Any time of the year but likely will peak around the busy spring selling season or the popular vacation rental times in your area

Safety issues: Personal safety issues related to working alone, with strangers, and in unfamiliar locations. You'll also be responsible for the properties and their contents while you're working, which means you'll need to protect against theft or damage during your watch.

Marketing ideas and how to reach your potential customers: Stop by the offices of realtors and rental companies and offer your services for whatever they need. Be open to taking on a multitude of tasks on, and be sure to ask your customers for referrals or leads to other realty companies. Check in with these people throughout the busy season, as they might lose regular employees or gain unexpected work they need help with.

Build in special offers and package deals or create group sessions: Offer your clients an on-call type of service in which they can call you to check properties on the weekends or at times when they are away. Offer a repeat business discount, suggest a buy one/get one offer, or give your customers a referral discount when you get work from their recommendations.

Break it down and make it your own:

▸ Household, yard, and general maintenance chores

These are the same chores covered in previous sections, but in this case, you are doing the work at mostly unoccupied residences. Realtors want their properties to be at their best for showings, so someone needs to keep the grass trimmed, the flowers watered, and the furniture dusted. Landlords often have to deal with rental units that are left in shambles and need cleaning or repair before they can be rented out again.

▶ Open house sitting and sign placement

You've probably noticed the "for sale" signs popping up all over your community, and most of these homes will have at least two open houses scheduled for the weekend. The real estate agent cannot be everywhere at once, so he or she needs to hire someone to sit at the open house and put up and remove signs. Be aware, though, that you'll be responsible for the safety of the house while you're on duty.

▶ Staging assistant

Real estate agents stage homes to make them more appealing to buyers. If the home is occupied, the realtor will come in and eliminate many of the owner's belonging to make the home more neutral. If the home is unoccupied, the realtor will bring in furniture, artwork, and even fake groceries to make the home seem lived in. In either situation, a lot of carrying and lifting is done in the staging process, and you can find lots of work helping in this area.

▶ Rental clean out

This level of cleaning goes beyond the basic scrubbing and sprucing up. Many times renters will vacate their units suddenly and leave their personal belongings or unwanted items behind. Before the landlord can even get to cleaning, all this stuff needs to be removed. This can be a gross job, but you can also find a few treasures to sell or repurpose. If you've already helped a landlord with the basic cleaning, let him or her know you're willing to help with the bigger jobs.

Job Category: Vacation Home Helper

Does your part of the country offer seasonal attractions such as skiing, fishing, boating, hiking, or similar outdoor activities? If so, many vacation homes in your area are used just a few weeks or months out of the year. The owners of these homes most likely live at least a few hours away, and they need help opening, closing, cleaning, and stocking the cupboards before the guest's arrival. The work that needs to be done is similar to the previous cleaning and maintenance jobs listed for regular homes, but in this case, you'll be doing the work for owners that live elsewhere. In many cases, you'll have to work on an on-call basis in which the owners might call a few days before they plan to use the home. You'll be expected to have the work done and the home ready when they arrive.

Potential hourly price range: You can expect to charge $10 per hour for basic cleaning, yard work, and grocery shopping. More detailed work such as home maintenance, deep cleaning, and winterizing can be charged at $15 to $20 per hour. Many helpers charge an overall fee instead of an hourly rate and set the fee by the level of caretaking needed. For example, preparing a large vacation home for a big party can be charged out at a one-time $150 fee. Smaller weekly lawn mowing while the owners are away can be charged at a $30 to $50 fee based on the size of the lawn. Check with local home maintenance companies, and set your fees at the lower end of their ranges.

> ## TIP!
>
> Because your client does not live near you, it might be difficult to collect your paycheck. Until you've established a good pay history with the client, set up an escrow account through your bank or use a service such as PayPal® to collect your money.

Equipment or supplies needed: The equipment you need depends greatly on the type of work you'll be doing. If you're buying groceries for the cabin, you'll need a car. If you're doing lawn work or cleaning, you'll need all the necessary equipment and supplies for those jobs. In this case, you can't depend on the supplies being at your work site. You'll also need a phone or laptop with Internet service, so your clients can reach you at the last minute.

Costs: Medium to high depending on the equipment you need

Logistical considerations: You'll need reliable transportation and the ability to travel to your work's location. You'll also have to be somewhat on call and be able to adjust your schedule to meet your client's needs.

Permits/licenses needed: None

Skills and education needed: You'll need knowledge of whatever work you are doing — from cleaning to yard work to home maintenance. Be sure to spell out exactly what chores you can perform for the client and keep a list of people who can help you to complete the remaining jobs.

Fits with these interests and attributes: Problem-solving skills, excellent attention to detail and ability to follow directions, good people skills, independent work-style

Your customer's profile:

Personal: Your customer is the owner of a vacation home, most likely does not live nearby, and needs help with keeping the property maintained. You can also find customers who prefer to show up to their vacation home and not lift a finger — they'll expect the cupboards to be stocked, the heat or AC turned on, the beds made, the lawn mowed, and so on. You also might have customers with vacation homes they rent out, and they'll need these chores to be done before the arrival of renters. *Rental property was covered briefly in the previous section titled "Realtor's or Landlord's Helper."*

Business: As mentioned previously, you can find work through Realtors® or property management companies that handle rentals for homeowners. You might also find overflow work during the busy season from home maintenance companies.

Sidebar

Do you have seasonal businesses in your area that cater to tourists? Many times these owners will leave the area after the season ends. If so, they might also need help to open up, shut down, or keep an eye on their businesses in the off-season.

References needed: Yes, but minimal — your work will prove your value.

Seasonality: Any time of the year but will peak during the tourist season in your area. Heavy maintenance chores will also increase at the beginning and end of the season, as homeowners need to winterize or open up their homes.

Safety issues: Personal safety issues related to working alone, in remote locations, or with strangers. Your customer's home or belongings could be damaged if you do your work improperly or if you neglect your duties such as turning the water off so the pipes don't freeze. You'll also be given the keys to the home, which means it will be your responsibility to make sure everything is securely protected and locked up when you're done. Keep your client's information private, and don't tell your friends or social network where you will be working — tell your parents, though, so they know where you are.

Marketing ideas and how to reach your potential customers: Start by talking with local Realtors — out-of-town owners often work with real estate companies to rent out their property. Be prepared with references. Post fliers in local hardware stores, grocery stores, or hobby shops where vacationers might stop while in town. Spread the word through your parents' friends or people you know that own vacation property.

Build in special offers and package deals or create group sessions: Offer the widest range of services with the least amount of hassle — even if it means sending jobs to other people. Team up with a group of trustworthy friends who can handle all the needed chores. If your clients know they can depend on you to get everything done, they'll give you repeat business and refer you to their friends.

Break it down and make it your own

Every household, cleaning, lawn, or personal service listed in previous sections also fits in this category. Think about the work that needs doing around a home and offer this service to those with vacation homes. Remember that your customers just want to show up at their vacation home, kick back, and relax. Give them peace of mind and an easy arrival, and you will get continuous work. Start with these job ideas, and you will find plenty of work:

▸ Season opening service.

Offer a service that includes a deep cleaning, airing out, minor maintenance, and everything else needed to open up the home for the season.

▸ Ongoing check-in service.

When the home is shut up, things still can go wrong, such as a pipe breaking or limb falling on the roof. You can offer a weekly inspection service in which you check the property to make sure everything is OK and take care of any problems that pop up.

▸ Season closing service.

For seasonal-use homes, a lot of work needs to be done before the house can be shut up safely. You can help put away all the equipment, make sure all the utilities are shut off properly, and take care of any end-of-year repairs.

▸ Arrival and departure service.

You can make sure the home is freshened up, the cupboards are stocked, the boats or other gear are ready to use, and the lawn is mowed. When the owners or renters leave, you can come in, clean up, and make sure everything is stowed away.

▸ Rental liaison.

Vacation homeowners that rent their properties out also need help connecting with incoming renters. You can offer a service in which you meet the renters, help them get settled, be available for assistance, and inspect the property after they have left.

Job Category: Boat, Recreational Vehicle, and Camper Maintenance

Chapter 4 covered the mechanical aspect of RV and boat work such as engine repair, but additional chores are needed to store these toys away properly for the winter or get them ready for the new season. Most people wait until the end of the season to do repairs, and they can use help with cleaning and minor maintenance. Many of these recreational items also need specific work such as

draining water systems or repainting the boat hull. Leaving these chores undone can lead to expensive damage.

Potential hourly price range: You can expect to charge $10 per hour for basic cleaning, $15 per hour for more advanced maintenance, repair work, or winterizing.

Equipment or supplies needed: This will depend on the type of work you're doing, but in most cases, your customers will have the necessary supplies to get the job done. You might want to carry your own cleaning gloves, extra long extension cord, and eye/ear protection.

Costs: Zero to low

Logistical considerations: You'll need transportation to get to the location where your customers store their boat or camper.

Permits/licenses needed: None unless you are driving your customer's vehicle, in which case, you'll need the proper license. There might be restrictions on the size of vehicle you can drive as a teen or with the type of vehicles allowed on your regular driver's license. Check with your local license bureau for more information.

Skills and education needed: You'll need basic cleaning or maintenance knowledge of the type of boat or camper you are working on. You might be expected to drive or move the RV or boat, so you'll need experience in attaching a trailer, parking large equipment, and so on.

Fits with these interests and attributes: Good attention to detail and ability to follow directions, like to help others, independent work-style

Your customer's profile:

Personal: Your customer is the owner of a boat, camper, or RV that is only used for a few months out of the year. They'll usually hire you to work with them to complete the chores needed to clean out at the end of the year and open up or de-winterize at the beginning of the season.

Business: You can find overflow work at bigger campgrounds or marinas as these sites provide clean-out services to their customers.

References needed: Yes, but minimal — your work will prove your value.

Seasonality: Work will be available near the end of the camping or boating season and again at the beginning of the boating season. You might find occasional repair or cleaning work while the season is in progress.

Safety issues: Personal safety issues related to working alone, with strangers, with large equipment, or in an unfamiliar location. There's also the potential of damage to your customer's belongings if the work is done improperly.

Marketing ideas and how to reach your potential customers: Post fliers at big campgrounds or marinas listing the services you can help with. Talk with storage facilities in your area and ask them to pass your name on to their customers. You can also try showing up in work clothes on the weekends. You'll always find someone working on his or her boat or RV, and he or she might be willing to hire you for a couple hours of work. Boating and camping enthusiasts are a tight-knit community, so ask for references and referrals.

Build in special offers and package deals or create group sessions: Offer your customers a full complement of services, even if it means sharing work with a few of your friends. If you're good at cleaning and your friend is mechanically inclined, you can offer a service in which you scrub the camper down while he winterizes the engine and plumbing systems.

Break it down and make it your own

▸ **Camper or RV maintenance**

By the end of a full camping season, every camper or RV is a little beat up and a lot dirty. From emptying out the cupboards to scrubbing down the exterior, a thorough cleaning is essential before the camper can be put to bed for the winter. Most owners empty their campers of everything including linens, dishes, and seat cushions. They'd love a helper to haul these things out and put it all back together before the next camping season. You can also help with touching up paint scuffs, patching any torn upholstery, and repairing minor damage done during the summer.

▸ Boat maintenance

Many large boats such as sailboats or cruisers are just floating campers. The boats need as much end-of-season cleaning as a camper. You can help carry things out, touch up any minor repairs, and give the boat a good cleaning before it is put away for the winter. The exteriors of boats also need extra care, and most boat owners have to sand and reseal the hulls of their boats every two or three years. It's a dirty and time-consuming job that is perfect for a hard-working teenager.

TIP!

Before you put the boat or camper away, scatter a dozen scented dryer sheets around its interior. Mice hate them, so they will stay out, and the camper will smell fresh when it is reopened in the spring.

Job Category: Errand Helper

Even after the house is cleaned and the grass is cut, the to-do list can still be a mile long and hard to finish. Being available to help with simple errands such as dropping off the dry cleaning or picking up groceries can  be a valuable service, and you can make a good amount of money.

Potential hourly price range: You can expect to charge $10 per hour plus mileage if you are driving your own vehicle.

Equipment or supplies needed: You don't need any equipment to run errands except a dependable mode of transportation. If the errands are nearby, you can probably get it done on bike or by foot, but the job will be much easier if you have a car.

Costs: High if using your own vehicle

Logistical considerations: You'll need reliable transportation and a good map or GPS to help you find your way around. You'll need to negotiate with your clients regarding mileage reimbursement if you are using your own vehicle. However, you'll have to able to assert yourself to make sure your customer isn't giving you more work than what you've negotiated. Establishing an acceptable time frame or charging per task will help you avoid taking on too much.

Permits/licenses needed: None unless you'll be driving your own or your customer's car. In this case, you'll need a driver's license and proper insurance coverage. Check with your parents and your customer to make sure you have the necessary policy to cover you while driving.

Skills and education needed: This job requires nothing more than simple common sense, good organizational skills, and the ability to work with people.

Fits with these interests and attributes: Problem-solving skills and the ability to do many things at once, good attention to detail, ability to follow directions, like to help others, independent work-style

Your customer's profile:

Personal: Anyone that needs help getting things done. Focus on big families or those with small children. You can find work from those in a temporary time-crunch due to a big life event such as a wedding or graduation party. Older people can often use help — sometimes their adult children will hire you.

Business: Small business owners also can use help getting their business or personal errands done especially during the times of year when their business is busy.

References needed: Yes, but minimal — your work will prove your value.

Seasonality: Any time of the year

Safety issues: Personal safety issues related to working alone or with strangers

Marketing ideas and how to reach your potential customers: Spread the word through your parents' group of friends or talk with people in your neighborhood. The more people you tell, the better your chances of finding work. Once you land a few jobs and do them well, be sure to ask for references and referrals for more work.

Build in special offers and package deals or create group sessions: Offer your customers a discount for repeat business or referrals that lead to work. Once you've worked for someone, come up with additional ways they can hire you. Make it easy for them to give you work. If you can manage it, try taking on multiple clients and combining their errands into one trip. For example, if you have three customers that need dry-cleaning errands, schedule all three pick-ups for the same time at the same dry cleaner.

Break it down and make it your own

▶ Everyday errand helper

These tasks can be everything from picking up a week's worth of groceries to running the dog to the groomer. Typically, your customer will expect you to give them two or three hours in one day and they'll give you a list of tasks to be accomplished.

▶ Big event errand helper

Anyone throwing a big party or event — either at home or at a separate venue — can use help getting things picked up, delivered, and handled. You can run to the paper supply store, the chair rental place, and so on. Be prepared to handle stress because your customer will expect you to handle your chores independently and cannot accept mistakes. People throwing big events also need help with their everyday errands, so make sure to offer this additional service.

▶ Birthday and anniversary service

People still love to send presents and cards to their friends and family, but staying on top of this monthly chore can be difficult. You can offer to keep a running calendar of special days, send reminders to your customers, and even buy cards and presents. Offer to package, address, and mail these cards and gifts. The best part of this job is you can do it well in advance and handle multiple customers at once.

Job Category: Scrapbook, Photo, or Recipe Organizer

Adults do not want to give up things like scrapbooking, making photo albums, or collecting recipes, but often, everyday life interferes with the time needed to keep up. Sometimes, too, people enjoy just one part of the hobby, such as gluing down the scrapbook pieces, but don't enjoy sorting through paper for the right piece. You can take over the overwhelming parts of the job and leave the rest to your customer.

Potential hourly price range: You can expect to charge $10 per hour.

Equipment or supplies needed: You should be able to use your customer's equipment and supplies to do just about any job. If you're attached to a certain pair of scissors or other crafting supply, you might want to bring along your own kit.

Costs: Low if working off site, high if providing your own computer

Logistical considerations: Transportation to your client's location

Permits/licenses needed: None

Skills and education needed: You'll need some basic scrapbooking or document-handling knowledge. These skills can be picked up easily from books at your library, Internet crafting websites, or by taking one of the free Saturday morning classes offered at large craft stores such as Hobby Lobby®.

Fits with these interests and attributes: Good attention to detail and an eye for graphic design, ability to handle repetitive tasks, independent work-style

Your customer's profile:

Personal: Your customer is anyone with a pile of photos, mementos, or recipes they've been meaning to organize and file. You can also find work with people who want to make a scrapbook gift for friends and family or for a special occasion.

Business: Many businesses also like to keep a yearly scrapbook or album of the company's accomplishments. You can work with them to collect these items throughout the year and pull it all together for their holiday party.

References needed: Yes, but minimal — your work will prove your value.

Seasonality: Any time of the year

Safety issues: Personal safety issues related to working alone or with strangers. You'll also be handling irreplaceable family pieces so there's the potential for damage to these belongings.

Marketing ideas and how to reach your potential customers: Spread the word through social networking sites and post pictures of projects you have completed. Make sure these photos don't show personal information. Put up fliers at craft supply stores offering your services as a "scrapbook assistant." Ask for referrals after you have completed a project. If it's OK with your customer, include a small card with your finished pieces listing your name and phone — such as "Scrapbook made by John Smith."

Build in special offers and package deals or create group sessions: Offer discounts for multiple projects for the same family. For example, make a scrapbook for the family to keep and a scrapbook for them to give to the grandparents. Offer a monthly or quarterly service in which you return to help clean up photos or recipes that have accumulated during that time.

Break it down and make it your own:

In addition to simple cleanup and organization of mementos, you can create a job out of handling specific event-related scrapbooking such as these:

▸ Special event photo boards or digital displays

You've seen these memory boards or running videos at just about every wedding, bar mitzvah, or graduation you have been to. Collecting the needed photos and mementos and putting them together is a huge undertaking — and most brides or mothers are too overworked to take this project on. You can set up a meeting with the family to select the pieces to include, take on the organizing and display effort, and create a beautiful piece they will treasure for years.

▸ Funeral displays or boards

Most families now put together a memory board to display at the funeral home. These boards are a big comfort to the mourners but require a lot of work from the family at a time when they're occupied with more important duties. Funeral homes frequently offer a service to create the boards for the families, and you could work with the funeral director as an independent contractor to create these pieces. In most cases, you won't need to meet with the family, and the funeral home will handle gathering the photos, mementos, and needed supplies for you to work with.

▸ Special occasion scrapbooks

Many families are spread across the country now, and they use scrapbooks or photo books as a way to share their special moments with friends and family members. Even something as simple as a family vacation or a new puppy can be an event they would like to commemorate. You can help with this job by collecting the materials and creating the books they will send out to family. Most online photo-sharing sites such as Shutterfly® offer services you can use to create and print these books easily from their websites.

▸ Recipe organization and cookbook creation

Anyone who clips and collects recipes has a stack of recipes they've been meaning to file. Some people like to put them in a recipe box while others prefer creating a digital version with links and searchable titles. A few hours on a Saturday could be enough to wade through the stack of recipes and get them organized into a usable system. You could also take the family's favorite and most used recipes and create a printed cookbook. The printing can range from simple photocopies to a "real" book created through online websites such as CreateMyCookbook (**http://createmycookbook.com**).

Job Category: Delivery or Messenger Service

Even with big players such as the U.S. Postal Service (USPS®) or FedEx® in the market, the little guy still has room to make money delivering important packages, business documents, and even store-bought products. People frequently leave paperwork until the last minute and then need it delivered right away. Others like the uniqueness of having invitations or special packages

hand-delivered. Some people don't want the hassle of hauling things to the post office or need assistance in packaging their items up. You can offer one niche such as business messenger service or a full range such as packaging, addressing, and delivering packages door-to-door.

Potential hourly price range: You can expect to make an average of $10 to $15 per hour, but most delivery services charge per item, by package size, by distance delivered, and by the time needed for delivery. Urgent deliveries or fragile packages can be charged the highest rates. Call a few delivery services in your area and ask for a rate sheet. Use this sheet to set your own rates and range of services; make sure to choose a rate at the low-end of the price ranges you find.

Equipment or supplies needed: In large cities where businesses are located closely together, you can develop a delivery route that is accessed easily by bike or by walking. You'll need a dependable and sturdy bike, a bike helmet, a bike lock to secure your bike during deliveries, appropriate clothing for the elements, and a basket or messenger's bag to hold your deliveries. If you're delivering by car, you'll need a reliable vehicle and a good map or GPS to find your way around the area. A cell phone or laptop with Internet access is ideal here because it gives you the fastest connection to customers. You'll need a receipt book or clipboard with signature sheets to record pick-up details, delivery addresses, and receiver's confirmation.

Costs: Low if using a bike, high if using a car

Logistical considerations: You might have to be ready to go at a moment's notice because many business documents need to be picked up and delivered within a short time. You'll be expected to pay for your own gas if using a car for deliveries — be sure to factor this cost into your prices. Set limits ahead of time regarding when you will work, where your delivery range covers, and what type of packages you will or will not handle. For expensive or irreplaceable items, require your customer to purchase shipping insurance offered through the shipping company.

Permits/licenses needed: If you're driving, you'll need a driver's license and proper insurance coverage. Check with your parents to make sure you have the necessary policy. Some cities also require yearly bike licenses or permits. Check with your local city hall for requirements.

Skills and education needed: Know your way around the area you're covering, have good driving, maneuvering, and parking skills to handle traffic on busy streets, and have skills in handling and protecting important packages while they're in transit.

Fits with these interests and attributes: Ability to handle stressful situations and short deadlines, reliability and trustworthiness, good organizational skills and attention to detail, people skills and ability to keep a secret, independent work-style

Your customer's profile:

Personal: Your customer can range widely from a homeowner with urgent legal documents to the grandma getting birthday presents off to her grandchildren.

Business: The business customer is one that handles many documents requiring urgent signatures or papers such as lawyers, insurance agents, bankers, or money managers. You can also find business customers that need delivery of the products they sell — such as auto parts, building supplies, or items sold through classified ads.

References needed: Yes, especially if handling important documents. Start out with small, less important deliveries and work your way, making sure to collect references from each customer as you go.

Seasonality: Any time of the year but might peak around the holidays, at tax time (April 15), or at the end of each fiscal quarter

Safety issues: You'll be handling irreplaceable, important documents so there's the potential for loss or damage to your customer's item. You will be expected to protect the confidentiality of all your customers, their deliveries, and the information contained in these documents. You'll also have the personal safety issues related to working alone, with strangers, in unfamiliar surroundings, and from driving on busy streets. Wear your seat belt or bike helmet, never go through a neighborhood you feel is unsafe, and make sure someone knows where your deliveries are taking you, the approximate time of your work, and the routes you'll be taking.

Marketing ideas and how to reach your potential customers: You're going to have a lot of competition especially in big cities, so you have to make yourself stand out. Pricing will be your first marketing edge — you have much lower overhead than the competition, so you can make money, even at low prices. Put up fliers with your prices and delivery guarantee in the coffee shops or diners that business people frequent. Stop by the receptionist desk of large businesses and drop off information about your messenger service. Be friendly and courteous, and introduce yourself to the people at your end-delivery sites. Be sure to leave your information with them, too, as they might have their own delivery needs.

> ### TIP!
>
> If possible, map out your pick-up and deliveries ahead of time so you can group your stops together and avoid wasting gas or time due to backtracking.

Build in special offers and package deals or create group sessions: Offer a delivery guarantee such as "Your package delivered on time or it is free!" Give your customers reduced rates for more than one package if grouped together in one delivery. Offer a repeat business or referral discount if the referral leads to new business.

Break it down and make it your own:

▸ Delivery plus packaging service

In addition to delivering packages, you can also offer your customer services to wrap and box their items. Fragile gifts, bulky products, or things that require special handling can be difficult for the average person to package.

Create your own packaging station stocked with boxes, bubble wrap, and packaging tape, so you add this valuable service to your base fee. Check with the shipping company you are using for their packaging guidelines, and ask if they offer free boxes.

▸ Invitation hand delivery

You've probably seen the over-the-top invitations delivered for Sweet 16 birthday bashes, weddings, or other big events. These hand-delivered invitations are a special way for the hosts to kick-off their celebrations. Offer your services to go door-to-door or office-to-office delivering these special invites. If you're really motivated, you can offer to dress the part for themed parties or make the invitations for your client.

Job Category: Child Care or Babysitting

Every parent you know can use a break from the kids — from babies to preteens. You have the energy and enthusiasm to keep the kids occupied. Of course as a babysitter, you're completely responsible for the  well-being of the little angels while they are in your care. This means that you'll have to take care of everything from changing diapers to giving baths to preparing meals to dealing with temper tantrums. With proper training and a little experience, though, you'll get used to these parts of the job.

Potential hourly price range: The going rate for child care ranges widely across the country. Most families pay a base rate between $5 and $15 per hour and then add extra for more than one child or for unusual circumstances, such as overnight stays. Ask your parents what they pay, or ask your friends who have babysitting jobs, and set your rates accordingly. Most people pay their sitters at the end of the day or week.

Equipment or supplies needed: In most cases, you'll have whatever you need at the home where you are working. If you really want to win over the kids, bring a bag filled with games, craft projects, or other fun activities. Wear comfortable clothes and shoes you're not afraid to get dirty. Having a cell phone along is nice but not necessary — and be sure to leave your phone in your pocket while you are working.

Costs: Zero to low

Logistical considerations: In most cases, the parents will pick you up and bring you home, but you can offer to provide your own transportation.

Permits/licenses needed: None, but most families would like you to have babysitter's training and first-aid certification. *Information on this training is shown at the end of this section.* If you'll be driving the children, be sure your driver's license allows passengers and they are covered with your car insurance policy.

Skills and education needed: You'll need basic first aid, safety, and child care knowledge — these will be covered in babysitter training sessions. You'll also need skills in handling temper tantrums or fights between siblings, knowledge in keeping the kids entertained, and minimal food preparation or cleaning skills. Before you take the job, discuss with the parents exactly what is expected of you while you're babysitting. Some parents will want you to prepare meals, clean up the house, and even throw in a load of laundry. Other parents want you to focus only on the kids and leave the rest for them to do later. Don't take on more than you're willing to do, and be assertive.

Fits with these interests and attributes: Love of kids, patience and empathy, ability to deal with and diffuse stressful situations, energetic and enthusiastic personality, good people skills

Your customer's profile:

Personal: Any parent with a child from birth through 12 years old. Your secondary customers are the children you are caring for — they might not hire or pay you, but they'll let their parents know if they want you to come back.

Business: You might be able to find work at day-care centers as a temporary fill-in for vacations or especially busy days.

References needed: Yes, most people will want to speak with others you have worked for and will want to see your Red Cross babysitter's certification.

Seasonality: Any time of the year but might peak on holiday weekends or during school breaks

Safety issues: The well-being of the children is your No. 1 concern, and you'll have to take on the responsibility of making sure the kids are in a safe environment. Kids are fast, and within an instant, they can dart into a street or put a small toy in their mouth. Vigilance is key when you are babysitting. You also need to ensure that you are personally safe if you're working in an unfamiliar neighborhood or with strangers. Occasionally, the parents you're babysitting for might return home after drinking, and it wouldn't be safe for you to ride with them — call your parents for a ride, even if it makes you uncomfortable.

Marketing ideas and how to reach your potential customers: Word-of-mouth is the best way to find customers because parents love to share names of their favorite babysitters. If you do a good job, you'll be rehired, and your name will be handed off to more customers. Ask your parents to tell their coworkers, friends, and neighbors that you're looking for babysitting jobs. Put up fliers at your grocery store with your name, phone number, and availability.

Build in special offers and package deals or create group sessions: Babysitting is tailor-made for bundling — gather a few of your friends, get together a few kids all at once, and everyone will have fun. Offer your best clients a special discount or gift at the end of the year. If you have special skills such as knowing a second language or the ability to teach music, you can combine this with babysitting for a value add-on — for a little extra fee, of course.

Break it down and make it your own:

Babysitting can be offered in a wide range of situations. If you don't want to change diapers, you can watch children that are potty-trained only. If you prefer older kids, you can offer to be a summer companion while the parents work. Of course, when you offer a broader range of services, you will get more work. Setting the parameters also can mean picking certain days, weeks, or hours you are willing to work. Here are a few suggestions for breaking down your babysitting services:

- Friday or Saturday date night. Keep a standing date with your customers to be available one night per month, so they can go out together.

- Saturday morning sitter. Parents of young children find it especially difficult to get all their weekend chores and errands done while dragging along a toddler. Offer to sit with the kids for a few hours in the morning so parents can get errands done.

- After school sitter. Many older kids are able to make their way home from school but still need someone to watch over them until the parents get home from work. If your school lets out earlier than the elementary schools in your area, you could meet the kids at the bus stop or at their home and hang out for a couple hours in the afternoon.

- Summer or school break day care. This can be a big job to take on but it will guarantee you have lots of work during your breaks from school. Make sure you can handle a whole day with the kids and that you will have adequate means of transportation during the day if you need to go somewhere.

- Kid chauffeur service. Older elementary kids and middle schoolers are always busy with after-school activities such as sports and music lessons, and they need to get back and forth to all these things. If you can drive, you could be their driver and sit with them at their activities. Just make sure you are OK driving kids who might be noisy and rambunctious. The bonus here is you can do your homework while you are waiting on the kids.

TIP!

If you are offering a "standing arrangement" to be available on a certain day, be sure to confirm with your customer at least one week before the night you're planning to work.

▸ Emergency or on-call fill-in service

If you have a flexible schedule, you can offer customers a drop-in service for when their children are sick. Day-care centers and schools do not allow kids to come when they are sick, but parents still might need to go to work. Of course, you'll have to deal with sick kids, so be sure this is something you can handle. You can also find work as a fill-in when their regular day-care center is closed for time off or maintenance issues.

▸ Mini-day camps

Similar to camps mentioned in previous sections, you could join with a few friends to offer a day camp for kids during their school breaks. You can offer crafts, activities, or whatever interests you and your friends. Make sure you have adequate space both indoors and outdoors and lots of patience to handle silly kids.

▸ Event sibling watcher

Younger siblings get hauled all over to sit and watch big sister or brother play sports, perform at concerts, and so on. The parents would love someone to watch them for the few hours of the performance. Once again, you can team up with a few friends and put together a babysitting service based on the sports calendar for your school. Some parents might be willing to pay you to watch the kids at the same venue as the event.

How to become a certified babysitter

In most communities, The American Red Cross (**www.redcross.org**) offers a babysitter training program that will teach you to care for kids of all ages. This hands-on class is geared toward 11- to 15-year-olds and lasts for about six and a half hours divided over a few Saturdays. You will come away with tons of knowledge including basic first aid and child-focused CPR, general kid hygiene and safety rules, baby care including diaper changing and feedings, and lessons on how to communicate effectively with parents. You'll receive a babysitter's handbook filled with additional ideas and helpful hints for your babysitting career. Parents look for this training when hiring a sitter, and you will be much more confident after taking these classes.

Most of these classes are offered through community education programs, and you might have to pay a minimal fee. If you can't find a class in your area, you can download most of the resources from the Red Cross website. This website also has lots of additional resources to review and print out, such as a resume template, a family interview card, a safety inspection checklist, and more. Visit the website and click on the "Take a Class" tab, then click on the "Caregiving and Babysitting" link.

Job Category: Adult Companion

Older people or those recovering from illness or surgery need assistance with everyday activities such as meal-preparation, home chore assistance, and general care. They might not be able to drive, so they need help getting to the grocery store, medical appointments, or social events such as card club. Sometimes, they just need someone to check on them and spend a little time with them. In most cases, your customer will have a home health aide or professional caregiver to handle hygiene and medical needs. By providing this service, you will help your  customer retain his or her dignity and independence and avoid leaving his or her home for a care facility. At first, you might feel uncomfortable around the old or the sick, but after a few afternoons, you'll probably find you have made a good and trusted friend with some great life lessons to share.

Potential hourly price range: You can expect to charge approximately $10 to $15 per hour for basic companion needs. More advanced assistance can be charged a higher rate, and you can charge mileage if using your own car to run errands or drive your customer to appointments.

Equipment or supplies needed: You don't need much equipment to take on this job. A cell phone is convenient as a way for your customers to reach you.

Costs: Zero unless using your own car

Logistical considerations: You'll need reliable transportation and a vehicle that is easy for an older person to get in and out of.

Permits/licenses needed: None unless you'll be driving your or your customer's car. In that case, you'll need a driver's license and proper insurance coverage. Check with your parents and your customer to make sure you have the necessary policy to cover you and your passenger while driving.

Skills and education needed: You'll need knowledge of basic home skills such as cooking, laundry, cleaning, and minor chores. Have basic first aid and safety training. You might need a network of others you can call in for help such as a home repairperson, a lawn care helper, or a money manager. You don't need formal training in elder care, but it's helpful to educate yourself on the issues you might face with this job. Numerous books and magazines focused on this subject are available at your library, or search online for "caring for the elderly in their homes."

Fits with these interests and attributes: Empathy, patience, compassion, good people and conversation skills, attention to detail and organizational skills

Your customer's profile:

Personal: The person who needs your assistance is your primary customer. In many cases, though, the person hiring you might be the spouse, children, or other relatives who live far away or are unavailable to provide the needed care.

Business: You might be able to find work through nursing homes, long-term care facilities, or assisted living complexes. These places have their own staff to handle these tasks, but they sometimes hire independent contractors to help with overflow work.

References needed: Yes, people will want to check with others you have worked with. If this is your first job, ask a trusted teacher or adult in your life to vouch for you. After you have done well at your first job, be sure to ask for a reference.

Seasonality: Any time of the year, but the need might peak in areas where winter weather makes travel or going outside difficult.

Safety issues: As with babysitting, there are serious safety issues when you are in charge of another person's care. You'll need to ensure your customer is protected from falls, burns, and other hazards. If you're handling foods or medicines, you'll need to be sure the food is cooked properly and OK for them to eat and their medicines are properly dispensed. You'll have access to personal belongings and private information, which you must protect and keep confidential. If a relative is hiring you, be sure to discuss whom this information can be shared with.

You need to ensure you are personally safe if you're working in an unfamiliar neighborhood, with strangers, or with people who might have impaired judgment or behavior due to illnesses such as Alzheimer's. You might also be asked to carry heavy packages or even lift your customer into a wheelchair — if you're not strong enough to handle the load, you could get hurt. Never take on a job in which you are uncomfortable with the people or tasks.

Marketing ideas and how to reach your potential customers: Word-of-mouth is the best way to find customers because this is such a personal business. Ask your parents and grandparents to tell coworkers, friends, and neighbors you're looking for companion care jobs. If you do a good job, you will be rehired, and your name will get handed off to more customers. Put up fliers at your grocery store or at local churches with your name, phone number, and list of things you can help with. Stop by local nursing homes, physical therapy centers, or short-term care facilities and let them know you're willing to help with patients at their facility or after they go back home.

TIP!

Remember that although older people have difficulty with physical tasks, they are still strong in spirit. The tasks you're doing for them now are chores they have easily handled in the past, and it can be frustrating for them to give up control — especially if it seems like their children are hiring you as a "friend" to take care of them. Be careful how you approach these jobs so you don't offend your client, and take special care to respectfully involve them whenever possible.

Build in special offers and package deals or create group sessions: Offer new customers a discounted rate for the first visit or sell a package of visits such as "Schedule four weekly visits, get one week free." Give your current customers a bonus for referrals that lead to new work. Team up with friends to offer a wide range of services to the same customer — such as lawn care, home maintenance, or computer assistance.

Break it down and make it your own:

Similar to child care, you can offer a narrow service such as grocery shopping only or a wide range of services that covers every daily need. Review the following ideas as a way to set up your services:

- Daily visits. You could do this check-in service after school or in the evening. You would stop by to check on your clients, inquire if they need anything, take care of little chores they have for you, or just sit and talk with them for social interaction. In some cases, you might be the only person your client talks to that day.

- Backup care. Adults who are taking care of their older relatives frequently need a break for work or travel. You can fill in during these times and take over some or all the care normally provided by these adults.

- Weekly or monthly assistance. Instead of handling the daily needs, you could take on the chores that only need to be done weekly or monthly. These would include grocery shopping, paying bills and handling paperwork, setting up appointments, going to the beauty shop, and so on.

▶ **Grocery, home supplies, and personal needs shopper**

Group together shopping trips for all your clients and make just one trip to the store. You'll have to sort things before drop off, make sure to help your customers put away their items, and spend a little time visiting with them before you leave. You could could offer to accompany your customer on their shopping trips and assist with carrying items or handling the money — be prepared to deal with slow progress of those who have issues with mobility.

▶ Downsizing assistance

Older people who have lived in the same house for decades often decide to move into a smaller condo or apartment but have too many belongings to fit into their new home. They need help in sorting through their things, packing up what they want to keep, and disposing of or giving away items they no longer need. You can help them get settled and assist with unpacking.

▶ Event companion

Grandparents still love to attend their grandchildren's events but often find it difficult to get there and maneuver at the venue. You can be their driver and assistant to get them settled in the bleachers. Those who have been widowed still want to attend social events such as plays, concerts, museum exhibits, or art gallery openings but don't want to go alone or cannot drive themselves. Accompany these people to the performances, and they'll usually pay for your admission.

Job Category: Pet Care

Many people get busy with work and other activities and don't have enough time to care for their pets properly. You can step in and carve out a job that keeps you and the little critters happy. From walking the dog

to feeding the hamster to cleaning the aquarium, there are dozens of ways to make money through helping out with pets.

Potential hourly price range: You can expect to charge $10 per hour, per pet for basic care such as feeding or walking. More advanced tasks such as grooming and aquarium cleaning can be charged at $12 to $15 per hour. Emergency or on-call care such as watching a dog full-time while the owners are gone can be charged at $15 to $20 per hour. You also can develop a flat fee price system in which you charge a flat rate per service such as $5 for a half-hour walk or $15 for a dog bath. Check with pet care services in your area, and set your fees at the low end of their price range.

Equipment or supplies needed: The equipment you need depends on the type of services you're offering, such as nail clippers or bathing supplies for grooming or a sturdy leash for walking big dogs. You should be able to use your customer's equipment, but you might want to invest in your own gear so you're more comfortable with it as you are working. For dog walking or other outdoor work, you'll need a good pair of walking shoes and clothing appropriate for all weather conditions.

Costs: Zero if using your customer's equipment, low to medium if providing your own gear

Logistical considerations: You'll need transportation to your client's home. Expect to be covered with hair or be wet or dirty, and plan to walk at least two miles during your work time.

Permits/licenses needed: None

Skills and education needed: You'll need basic knowledge of how to care for and train the type of animal you're working with. You'll also need to know how to use the equipment such as an electric trimmer, nail clipper, or training collar. Your local library will have a book covering the necessities of pet care *if needed*. Make sure you don't take on a pet care job unless you know what you are doing.

Fits with these interests and attributes: Love of animals, patience, independent work-style, high energy, and enthusiasm

Your customer's profile:

Personal: Anyone with a pet that needs regular, daily care such as walking; temporary care during times the pet parent is away; or specialized services such as training or grooming. Your most likely customer will be a dog or cat owner, but you can also find work caring for exotic or unusual pets if you have experience with that species.

Business: You might find overflow work from pet stores, vet clinics, or boarding kennels during times when they are too busy to handle everything.

References needed: Yes, people will want to speak with previous customers or an adult who can attest to your ability to handle animals. If you have volunteered to watch a friend's or neighbor's pet, use them as a reference.

Seasonality: Any time of the year

Safety issues: Personal safety issues include working alone, with strangers, or in unfamiliar environments. The pets you are caring for can injure you if they are scared, jumpy, or unpredictable. You'll also be responsible for the safety and well-being of the animal and other people this animal might meet while you are outside. In some cases, you'll be given keys to the pet owner's home, so you'll be responsible for locking up when you're gone. Be careful about sharing information about your clients, especially if they're going away.

Marketing ideas and how to reach your potential customers: Spread the word through your neighborhood and other adults you know that you're interested in helping with their pets. Put up fliers at local stores or pet stores listing your name, phone number, and services you're willing to provide.

Build in special offers and package deals or create group sessions: If you can handle more than one dog at a time and you're sure they'll get along, consider walking two or more dogs at once. You'll be able to charge per dog, per hour, effectively doubling or tripling your hourly rate. Offer your customers a package deal such as "Buy four daily walks, get one day free."

Break it down and make it your own:

Pet care can be offered at various levels from full-service daily care to temporary dog walking during vacations. Set up your service to fit your schedule and the pet tasks you'd like to take on. Make sure you aren't charging friends and neighbors for things you normally would do free. Ask them, though, for references in finding new work.

▶ Daily walking, feeding, or check-up service

As much as pet parents love their animals, finding time to give them proper exercise and care can be difficult. Playtime, regular feedings, and a clean environment, though, are essential to the well-being of the animals. You can provide any or all of these services on weekdays while the family is away and let them take over on the weekend. If you know how to clean an aquarium or a hamster cage, offer this as a weekly or twice-a-month service.

CASE STUDY: ON THE JOB WITH BLAKE WRIGHT

Occupation: Dog walker
Age: Started her business at age 18

When it came time to choose a college, I was determined to go to my dream school — even if it meant paying out-of-state tuition. After my first year, though, I needed to make money, but jobs were scarce, so I decided to create my own. My big idea came to me one day when I was missing my dog back home. I decided to turn my love of dogs into a moneymaker by walking or running dogs for other people. It would be perfect for me because I lived downtown where people needed this service — plus I wouldn't need a car or gas money to get back and forth to work.

I started out by posting an ad on Craigslist and putting up fliers at a local dog park. I also hung fliers in well-to-do downtown areas where I knew people would be willing to pay to have their dogs walked. I started out charging $5 per dog for a 20-minute walk. So many people called from these initial ads that I ended up turning people down. I have found more jobs through word-of-mouth and referrals from current customers, which is essentially free advertising. Now that I'm more organized and experienced, I can walk up to five dogs at once; I am really making $25 for every 20-minute walk, which is much more money per hour than I would make at any other campus job. When I get super busy, I hand off my overflow work to some close friends, and they pay me half of what they make in exchange for my arranging the job.

Another advantage of this job is the only "materials" I need are my time and labor. Of course, if it rains, I'm out the money for that day and have no way to make it up. Working for myself also allows me to set my hours around my class schedule — which works very well for a full-time student. I have learned a lot of valuable lessons through working for myself, including knowing that I am capable of running a business and that I can succeed at making money.

Words of Wisdom: There are always ways to make money. Do something you'll enjoy, and make sure you are willing to stick to it.

‣ Overnight or vacation care

When owners are traveling, pets still need regular care, and some get anxious if left alone for a long time. Regular boarding kennels, though, can be expensive and overwhelming for pets. You can offer a less expensive service in which you either stay overnight with the pet or visit a few times a day to feed, water, and play with the pet. If it is OK with your parents and the pet's parents, you can offer to bring the pet to your house while they're away. Just make sure your siblings and pets will be safe around this new boarder.

‣ Grooming or training

People pay a lot of money to keep their pets' hair and nails trimmed. They also spend hours, money, or both taking puppies and adult dogs to basic behavior, hunting, or companionship classes. If you know training or grooming, you can set up your own service to take on these tasks.

‣ Non-traditional or exotic pet care

From parrots to tropical fish to snakes to pot-bellied pigs, if you're experienced with any specific animal, you can offer services for this species and charge a higher rate because of your advanced skill. You can also serve as a consultant for those considering purchasing this type of pet or for people new to ownership.

CHAPTER SEVEN

Make Money by Selling Things

The art of sales has been dissected and discussed since the first market opened in Ancient Greece. Sellers still are trying to understand what motivates people to buy and how to create irresistible products and marketing that appeals to customers. No matter what job you are doing as a self-employed teen, you're already a salesperson because you are convincing people to hire you. However, this job segment isn't only about selling yourself but also selling a product.

You probably won't become a millionaire, but if you can make or find something people want, you can put money in your pocket. You don't have to be a smarmy car salesman to succeed at sales — good people skills combined with a valuable product is all you need. Choose a product you are interested in and one that relates to your hobbies. When you believe in the product, it will show and will make it easier to convince others to buy it.

Selling products can be divided into two broad categories: used or repurposed items and handmade or new products. The first half of this chapter will cover used goods and the second half will cover new or handmade products. You'll have to find a way to get your product in front of customers. This can be done face-to-face or through market settings, through classified ads or garage sales, through the mail, online through your own website, or via sales sites such as Craigslist or eBay. You also can sell antiques, jewelry, or collectibles to antique dealers, home décor stores, or pawn shops — you must be 18 years old to use the services of a pawn shop. You'll have to spend some non-billable hours looking for the right outlet for your product. Start small and don't invest a lot of time or money before you're sure you can handle the demands of your production and that you have an adequate customer base to make money.

Making a sale is the end of the process, and before you make any money, you'll have to put in some legwork to get things ready to go. Make sure this is something worth doing by assessing the logistical considerations of how you will produce, store, and transport your product. Thinking about these issues beforehand will help you adequately estimate what is required to make money. As you're developing your business, think through every step needed to get your products into your customer's hands including:

- Production or product acquisition. How will you pay for your products or the raw materials to create your products? Where will you get the products you need for sales?

- Storage. Where will you store your products, and do you have the space and equipment to house everything while it is in process or between sales?

- Transportation. How will you get your products to the post office for delivery or to the markets? Do you have a big enough vehicle?

- Customer service. Do have a reliable way for customers to contact you, and do you have the time to answer quickly? Can you guarantee your products? How will you handle dissatisfied customers?

These considerations will be discussed in each section and covered in the book's remaining chapters. Most everything listed can be sold online. Chapter 8 will go into more detail on using Internet auction or sales sites.

Job Category: Selling Used, Repurposed, or Secondhand Goods

Used items can range from a truckload of scrap metal you've collected to expensive antiques you've unearthed to used video games. Many times, you can sell the items you find as is, with a hefty markup, of course. Used

items can also be repurposed or refinished to increase their value, such as sanding and refinishing an old table or remaking broken china into wall-hanging mosaics. If you're a fan of the TV shows *American Pickers*, *Cash & Cari*, or *Storage Wars*, you understand what sorts of treasures can be found and resold at a large profit.

You'll need to become familiar with the value of your items, so you know how much to pay and how to set your prices. As you begin, stick with a narrow segment of goods you are interested in and in which you have some background knowledge. Check your local library for books on these specific items and look for current guides with price listings. Another great place to find the market value of your item is on eBay. Once you are on the site, click the Advanced Search button, and then check the Completed Listings box. This will show listings that have ended with the final prices or will show if the item did not sell. You can go to a professional appraiser, but this will cost you money, even if the item turns out to be fake or not valuable. Look in your local yellow pages or stop by an antique store to find a reliable professional. Beware of "road show" appraisers that come to town for one-day shows. They typically appraise items low and offer you money on the spot when, in reality, you could sell your item elsewhere for a much higher price.

> ## TIP!
>
> When you're selling used or salvaged goods, you're not only making money but are also helping the environment by recycling products and keeping them in use instead of sending them to a landfill.

Potential hourly price range: Your hourly rate is determined by how much money is left after your expenses are met. This leftover amount then can be divided by the hours you put into creating or finding the product, refinishing or repairing it, and the time spent selling or delivering it. The more efficiently you use your time, the higher your profit will be. Most people set a price that is double the amount of what they paid for the item — this gives enough room to cover production and delivery costs and still offers a slim profit. Of course, your prices still will need to stay in line with the going market rate, or you won't find customers.

Setting the price on valuable or rare pieces can be tricky, and it is hard to know exactly how much something is worth. There's no UPC code on the bottom of a 100-year-old piece of china, and sometimes the price is whatever the market will pay. In these instances, an auction can be the best way to sell collectibles because the buyers will set their own price. You can often put a reserve price when listing a piece through auction, which means if the bids do not reach this price, the piece won't sell. Thoroughly researching your treasure and finding two or three price estimates or final sale prices will help you find an appropriate starting price for your piece. Be prepared to haggle with customers when selling at a market. You can also decide how much profit you are willing to take and set your price at this level even if it is below the "going rate."

Equipment or supplies needed: Your equipment needs will vary with what you're selling. You might need refinishing tools, a big truck to haul your products, production equipment such as a stove or art studio, display stands or a digital camera to showcase your products, and packing or delivery supplies for transport. Your job will be easier if you have a smart phone or laptop computer with Internet access — both for checking values and finding customers.

Costs: Medium to high if using your own equipment. You'll also need up-front money to purchase items or raw materials, pay for refinishing costs, or pay for advertising or listing fees. As you start making sales, be sure to set some money aside for future purchases.

Logistical considerations: In most instances, you'll need a large vehicle for transporting your goods both from where you purchased it and to bring it to market or delivery. Collecting these secondhand items can be a dirty, backbreaking job, and many times you will come home empty-handed. You might also have to spend many hours looking for items to sell.

Permits/licenses needed: None

Skills and education needed: You'll need knowledge of the product you're selling — such as where to find it, how to make it, and the item's potential value and market desirability. You'll also need the skills to make the item presentable for sales, including cleaning or refinishing, packaging, or displaying the item. Depending on where you're buying your products, you might need negotiating skills and the ability to haggle with the seller.

Fits with these interests and attributes: Curiosity and the desire to hunt for treasures, negotiating and people skills, salesmanship, communication skills, creativity, independent work-style

Your customer's profile:

Personal: Anyone with money in need of what you're selling. Your customer can be a collector looking for more pieces but also can be someone who doesn't know they need your product until they see it displayed.

Business: If you're selling something unique or hard-to-find such as framed art prints or office decor, you might also find businesses interested in purchasing your goods. Consignment stores, antique shops, or flea market vendors are a good secondary market for your products — and they can be a good partner if they're offering to share or rent selling space.

References needed: None, your product will speak for itself.

Seasonality: Any time of the year

Safety issues: Personal safety issues related to working alone, with strangers, or in unfamiliar settings such as flea markets. If you're meeting privately with customers to sell products, you could be put in an unsafe situation. Bring a friend or adult along, and make sure someone knows where you are going. You can also put yourself in danger when looking for products such as going into rickety old barns or sorting through the materials with sharp metals.

Marketing ideas and how to reach your potential customers: List your products online or set up a booth at sales markets such as weekend farmers markets or antique malls. You can also throw your own garage sale or post classified listings in your local paper. For specialty items such as video games or sports equipment, spread the word through the groups of people who would be most interested in these items. If possible, keep a list of previous customers so you can contact them when you get new inventory.

Build in special offers and package deals or create group sessions: Team up with friends who are also selling similar but different items, and travel to a few markets in the summer. Offer your customers a free trial or bonus package when they order. If you're selling more than one product, give them a free sample of the item they are not buying. If your products are seasonal, market your product as "limited time offer" to get people excited.

Break it down and make it your own

Your product inventory can be found anywhere — your own closet or attic, your neighbor's garage, local secondhand stores such as Goodwill®, or farm auctions listed in your local paper. Auctions and garage sales can feel like a strange environment, but the people are nice and love to see a young person taking an interest — just mind your manners, pay attention to what is happening, and ask questions if you're not sure. After your first few sales, you will get the hang of it and be ready to dive right in.

If you're willing to dig, have some seed money to start out with, and have an eye for value, you'll be able to find more than enough to stock your tables or online listings. Try to focus on one narrow segment at first, or you will become overwhelmed with handling your products and listings. Here are a few ideas of items you can find and resell at a good profit:

▸ Antiques, collectibles, and treasures

If it's old, rare, or unusual, someone out there wants to buy it. The range of salable items can be anything from antique furniture to rare coins to vintage kitchenware to old toys. People even collect things like bedpans and airline barf bags. The items don't need to be priceless antiques to have value. Do a quick search on eBay under "vintage toys" or "vintage china," and you'll see how much the collectible market covers. If you can find the pieces people are looking for and connect with them, you will make money. You just need to acquire these pieces at a good price so you have enough room for profit. Stay focused on what you know and only buy things with good potential.

You have many options when it comes to selling your item, and it depends on how much time you want to put into sales. You could sell your items online through eBay or similar auction sites. You could travel to local flea markets, collector fairs, or antique shows and set up a table for sales. You also can place your items in consignment shops, galleries, or antique stores.

All of these options require a fee or commission, so be sure to factor that in your price.

▸ Household items, outdoor equipment, sports gear, clothing sales, and everything else

From clothing to sports equipment to baby toys, people always are looking for a bargain in this area. Kids outgrow clothing and sports gear, adults move on to other hobbies, and older people are trying to downsize, but these belongings still have plenty of use left in them. You probably can find enough in your own home to have a great starter sale, and your parents will love to get the closets cleaned out. Host your own garage sale or put your stuff in consignment or secondhand stores. These used items also sell well through eBay or Craigslist — just be sure everything is clean, working, and in good condition. You also could offer your friends a deal in which you sell their stuff for a small percentage of the final sale price.

Do you have an old prom, homecoming, or other special event dress in your closet? You probably paid a lot of money for it and only wore it for a few hours, but it is still in fashion and wearable. Try selling it through the classifieds or gather up a bunch of dresses and host a Prom Boutique sale a couple of months before the big day. Make sure your dresses are mended and cleaned before your sale and list them at 40 percent of what you paid.

▸ Video games, gaming systems, electronics, and DVDs

These also are considered secondhand sales but are limited to the electronics department. Plenty of people would love to have your old electronics, and some items even might be considered vintage. You can usually find games, CDs, DVDs, and gaming systems at rummage sales or from your friends and can resell them online or through classified ads. Make sure everything is working and complete. Even if you make only $2 per game, it will not take long to add up. You also can try creating a rental or trading service such as:

- Gamer membership. Create a lending library of video games similar to Game Fly™ or Netflix®. You charge members a monthly fee, and they can "check out" one or two video games per month. Be aware, though, that games will be damaged more quickly than with normal one-player usage.

- Game or movie exchange club. Organize a monthly swap meet in which people bring in their used games to trade or sell to other games. You do the legwork and organization and charge a small entry fee for those belonging to the club. You can also be a buyer to find games to sell yourself.

- Game systems, stereos or MP3 players, televisions, and other electronics. A little more advanced than selling video games, you can build quite a business around reselling the electronics everyone has sitting in their homes. Whether the kids no longer play with the Wii® or the neighbors are downsizing and need to get rid of a TV, you can be the person to unhook it, haul it out, and find a buyer. You either can do this service for a percentage-of-sales fee or buy the equipment outright. If you or a friend knows how to fix broken electronics, you can also sell refurbished equipment after you have it back to working order. It is imperative, though, when you are selling electronics that you guarantee your product — your customer must know you will return their money if the item doesn't work.

▸ Repurposed or refinished items

Sometimes the treasures you find need a little attention before they can be resold. This can be as simple as a good cleaning with furniture polish or as complex as a complete refinishing or rebuilding. To get your ideas rolling, search online for "repurposed home decorating." To sell your creations, set up a booth at flea markets, craft fairs, or consider selling through online sites such as Etsy.

▸ Make your own sales market

A recent trend in repurposed or secondhand sales is the monthly or quarterly "seller's market" or "barn sale." These are a loose collaboration between like-minded sellers and are similar to a craft fair or flea market. The sellers work together to find a central location such as a big barn or shed and set up booths in the barn for a one- or two-day sale held every few months or once a year before big shopping holidays such as Christmas. The group shares minimal overhead costs such as advertising and space rental. The group also works together to set up and tear down, but you'll have to provide your own display tables and transport your products to the barn. These sales are a great way to reach new customers because the clients will come to the sale looking for a specific item, then browse through the other displays looking for more to buy.

▸ Scrap metal or aluminum sales

A scavenger-hunt way to make money might be to scour ditches or old sheds for scrap metal. You can also gather beverage cans and get paid for the aluminum. Recyclers buy most metals by the pound to be reused for construction or industrial purposes. For big scrap-metal piles, landowners will pay you for cleaning out their metal, and you can then sell that metal for a profit. To do this job, you will need a big truck, strong muscles, and a willingness to get dirty. You'll also have to sort and separate out each metal if it is attached to another material such as wood or plastic. This can be a dangerous job because you'll be handling heavy objects with sharp edges, so wear a good pair of work boots, sturdy gloves, and eye protection. To sell your salvaged metal, look in your local yellow pages under "scrap metal" or "recycling." Visit the Institute of Scrap Recycling Industries, Inc. (**www.isri.org**) for more details on metal recycling.

▸ Precious metals such as gold

The prices for gold, silver, copper, and nickel have soared in recent years and have turned finding these precious metals into a modern-day gold rush. You or your parents probably have an old earring, bracelet, or twisted necklace chain sitting in your jewelry box right now that is worth good money. A small 14-carat gold hoop earring can be worth nearly $20 in today's market. Older coins, vintage silverware, and even old cell phones contain gold or silver, though sometimes the value of the piece is higher than its metal content. Keep an eye out as you go to rummage sales for full jewelry boxes or silverware — sometimes you'll find hidden treasure at rock-bottom prices. Be sure to ask your parents before you raid your mom's jewelry box or sell your own jewelry.

You have numerous ways to tell if something is gold, but these tests can be expensive, complex, and require specialized equipment. For your purposes, the first thing to do is to look for markings on the piece. Jewelry will have a marking on the back listing the carat weight of the piece, and silverware will list the manufacturer and if it is silver plated. Another simple gold test is to use a medium-strength magnet because gold is non-magnetic and will not be drawn to the magnet. This is not foolproof, however, because counterfeiters can use other non-magnetic metals painted gold. Your appraiser or jeweler will perform additional tests to determine if the piece is gold and how much gold is present.

The best place to sell your jewelry, coins, or silverware is at a reputable jewelry store or pawnshop. They will give you an estimate of value and offer you immediate cash or store credit. Be sure to get a few different estimates before selling your gold, and avoid selling to companies who ask you to mail in your pieces for appraisal. Avoid, too, appraisers that come to town for one day or home gold-buying parties, as these companies pay the lowest rates.

Job Category: New or Handmade Products

Just like the big retailers or small Mom-and-Pop shops, you can make money by selling new or handmade products. The sky is the limit here, and your options are only reined in by your skills, your imagination, and your motivation to get out and make the sale. Previous chapters talked about harnessing your special talents to make money. This chapter will continue that discussion by showing you how to use your skills to make things to sell. Whether you can paint, bake, sew, or invent, plenty of money can be made in this segment. You can also sell already-made products as an independent consultant for big businesses such as PartyLite®. Additionally, if you've created the latest fad or invented something different, you might find businesses that want to buy the rights to your product or become your partner. *Chapter 11 will cover franchising, partnering, and other more advanced business situations.*

Potential hourly price range: Selling products in this manner isn't an hourly wage job. You can determine your potential wages by first deducting expenses from your total sales and then dividing the remaining amount by the time you put into manufacturing, selling, and delivering the product. You'll make the most money by being frugal with expenses and efficient with your time. To find a ballpark figure of how much you can expect to make, estimate the costs of production and marketing, time needed to sell, and the expected sales you think you can make. Most people set a price that is double the amount of raw materials — this gives enough room for a small profit. Of course, your prices will still need to be similar to your competition, or you won't find customers.

Equipment or supplies needed: Your equipment and supply needs will vary with what you're selling. You might need a big kitchen, an art studio, a workshop, or specialized tools. You'll need a way to transport your products to the sales site or delivery service and a method of displaying your wares, such as a folding table or shelving system. Your job will be easier if you have a digital camera, smart phone, or laptop computer with Internet access.

Costs: Medium to high if using your own equipment. You'll also need up-front money to purchase items or raw materials and pay for advertising or listing fees. As you start making sales, be sure to set some money aside for future production.

Logistical considerations: You'll need a space to store your products in between sales and a way to transport them back and forth.

Permits/licenses needed: If you're selling food items, you might need a local vendor's permit or food safety license. Check with your city hall or county extension office for information on the requirements for your area.

Skills and education needed: You'll need the skills to produce and package the item for sales. You'll need education in basic customer service, accounting, and tax issues.

Fits with these interests and attributes: Creativity and the ability to identify salable products, salesmanship, communication skills, independent work-style

Your customer's profile:

Personal: Your personal customer is anyone — young or old, homeowners or travelers, and anyone with an interest in what you're making. Most of your customers will find you through their shopping habits, either online or at local craft fairs or art galleries. The more you display your work or give out samples, the broader your customer base will be.

Business: Occasionally, a personal customer can become a business customer. For instance, someone might buy your muffins at a Saturday morning farmers market and then want to order a few dozen for their office meeting. You might also find business owners who want to buy art for their office space or who own galleries or consignment shops in which you can display your pieces.

References needed: None, your product will speak for itself.

Seasonality: Any time of the year but might peak around the season in which your product is most wanted, such as pumpkins at Halloween or candy on Valentine's Day

Safety issues: Personal safety issues related to working alone, with strangers, or in unfamiliar settings such as craft fairs. If you're meeting privately with customers to sell products, you could be put in a situation that is unsafe — bring a friend or adult along and make sure someone knows where you are going. If your work requires dangerous equipment such as a hot oven or sharp glass, you can be injured while working. If you're creating fragile artwork or perishable food items, your product can be damaged while in transit.

Marketing ideas and how to reach your potential customers: No matter what you are selling — even if it is a dozen eggs or fresh veggies — find a way to package and label your products so people can find you again if they want more. You must also create opportunities for "face time" so people can see, feel, smell, or taste your product. Book as many craft fairs or farmers markets as you can handle and always give out free samples. If you are selling online, describe your product as richly as possible, take good quality digital pictures, get reviews from previous customers, and offer a satisfaction guarantee.

Build in special offers and package deals or create group sessions: A great way to sell more of your product is to offer it in a premade gift basket. Put together a collection of your item, package it up with pretty ribbon, and even offer to deliver it for an additional fee. You can also offer your customers a small sample size of other products you sell or put together a "buy two, get one free" offer. If a friend is selling something different, work together to attend craft fairs, and you'll be able to split the costs of travel and entry fees. If you're motivated, you could put together your own sales fair such as the barn sale talked about in the previous section.

Break it down and make it your own

Next to producing or sourcing the product, your biggest concern is finding a place to sell your product. In many cases, you will have a built-in customer base that will need nurturing such as when you are selling with a home-based business. Homemade goods or artwork will require a lot of your time sitting at art shows or putting up listings on the Internet. As with selling used goods, it is best to focus on one narrow segment within your product line and grow your offerings as you learn more about your customer and the marketplace.

▸ Multi-level marketing companies or direct-to-buyer sales

From perfume to purses to kitchen equipment, hundreds of national companies are looking for salespeople to sell their products directly to buyers. These companies also sometimes are called network marketers or direct sales companies. They operate in nearly every segment of sales — some of the biggest players include The Longaberger® Co., The Pampered Chef®, Avon®, Stampin Up!®, and Arbonne®. You've probably been invited to one of these in-home shows hosted by a friend or relative in which they offer a few snacks, give a short presentation on the products, give out samples, and then encourage you to order right on the spot. Salespeople for these companies are considered independent contractors and work on commission. They also get bonuses or free products for signing on new salespeople or booking additional home parties.

In most cases, you must be 18 years old to sign on as a salesperson, but you could arrange to work with an adult and share the profits until you turn 18. These jobs do require a high degree of sales acumen. It can become awkward when you're selling things to your friends and they might feel like they have to buy something from you. These direct sales businesses, though, can be quite successful and easily can go with you when you move to college. The larger, established companies provide thorough training and assistance, so you'll learn a lot about running a successful business.

Before signing on to be a direct marketer, thoroughly research the company, and don't put money down on training or other administrative fees. The most reputable companies won't require you to buy product to sell later — they will ship product to you after you have received orders. Work through someone you know, and ask questions before you commit. Check the website for the Direct Selling Association at **www.dsa.org** for more information on the direct selling field, fact sheets on the industry, government regulations, a seller's code of ethics, and more.

▸ Homemade food items

People love to buy homemade food products, especially if they are unique or can help the family when making dinners. If you have a special family recipe, can make a delicious an ethnic dish, or just love to cook, you can make money by selling your home-cooked creations. *Chapter 4 covered the basics behind making money through food preparation.* The key point when cooking is to follow all food handling safety rules. You don't want to make your customers sick. The U.S. government site (**www.foodsafety.gov**) covers every food-safety related topic you will come across and is a great place to learn proper food-handling techniques. If you're preparing food in a public setting such as at a concession stand, you'll most likely need a food permit and basic food safety certification. Check with your local government office for more information.

Find outlets to sell your goodies by contacting local food co-ops or restaurants, through selling to friends and neighbors, or setting up a concession stand or table at local farmers markets or craft fairs. Your product will speak for itself, so give out free samples. If you are tech-savvy, you could set up a website and market your treats online. Make sure you can handle the demand and don't end up taking more orders than you can fulfill.

In most cases, you'll need to spend some money up front to buy ingredients and containers such as canning jars or muffin boxes. Ideally, your parents will let you use their kitchen and cooking equipment and might even chip in to fund your first batch. Once you have started making money, save some to pay for ingredients and packaging materials. Be sure to label your packages with your name, email, or phone number so people can order more from you. These labels are simple to make with any word processing program and can be printed at home on standard sticky-backed labels. Consider these fun ideas for easy-to-make goodies:

- Big cookies, muffins, cakes, or breads
- Candies and chocolates
- Jams, jellies, or specialty syrups
- Pestos, salsas, and sauces
- Pickles, sauerkraut, or canned goods
- Soup or spice dry mixes
- Ethnic specialties
- Frozen soups or casseroles that can be baked at home
- Smoothies or milkshakes

▶ Garden products

Do you have a green thumb or access to fresh produce, live plants, or animal products such as eggs? These are terrific sellers at farmers markets, local garden stores, or organic food shops, and if you put in the labor, you will have a wide profit margin. Your product line can be one item or cover the range of produce as it comes into season. Many of these products can be raised on a small piece of ground and don't require a lot of gardening know-how. You could also contact producers in your area and offer to sell produce for them. Visit your local farmers markets to see what most people sell, and consider bringing something different. You can sell just about anything that is homegrown including:

- Houseplants, landscaping plants, bushes, or trees
- Bulbs, tubers, or other plant cuttings such as hostas
- Fresh-cut flowers or greenery
- Fresh vegetables, berries, or fruit
- Eggs or honey

- Natural decorative items such as pumpkins, pinecones, or gourds

Don't forget to include your name and phone number on the package or bags. People might call you with large orders at canning time or around the holidays.

▸ Pet and animal products

People love their animals as much as they love their children and are happy to spend money on treats and gifts for their furry friends. If you're handy with a sewing machine or can bake a dog treat, you can make a selection of items for pet parents to splurge on. Stop by small craft stores, pet shops, vet offices, or hardware stores in your area and ask them to carry your items. Set up a table at local craft fairs or farmers markets showcasing your wares. Take pictures and gather testimonials from current customers, and post these on social media sites to spread the word. Get started with these ideas:

- Dog or cat treats. Search online under "dog or cat treats," and you will find hundreds of recipes for easy-to-make pet goodies.

- Pet clothing. You have seen the little "purse pooches" all the celebrities carry around, and these little doggies are always dressed up in the latest pet fashions. Look online for sewing patterns for simple pieces designed for all sizes of dogs — or create your own line of pet couture.

- Pet jewelry. Make fun collars or collar tags with a few simple supplies from your local craft store

- Beds or blankets. Every dog needs a place to sleep, and every dog owner needs a way to keep the dog hair off the sofa or backseat of the car. Sew up a soft, washable bed or seat cover, and your customers will be barking for more.

CASE STUDY: ON THE JOB WITH CHELSEY HOMAN

Occupation: Owner, Doggy Decadents
Age: started her business at age 18
doggydbakery@gmail.com
www.AKDogTreats.com

When I was 17, I had the opportunity to attend a teen entrepreneurship camp at Cornell University. This camp opened my eyes to the

Chelsey Homan with her product line. Photo courtesy of Chelsey Homan.

benefits of working for yourself, and I knew developing my own business would distinguish me from my peers when it came time to apply for college scholarships. I also looked at self-employment as my own personal internship and knew it would teach me how to build and operate a business on a

small scale without investing a lot of money. Working for myself also afforded me the flexibility I needed to manage my busy school schedule.

I first came up with the idea of baking dog treats when I was 17 and working at a pet store. I had been baking treats at home for my dog, Skipper, and thought others might enjoy home-baked treats for their pets. Before starting the business, I researched the dog bakery business and looked for some good recipes. I also researched packaging stores to find product bags and worked on developing a name and label for my products. I received some help from a friend to build my website and purchase a domain name. When I turned 18, I quit my job and started baking dog treats out of my parent's kitchen.

I took my products to local pet businesses in the hope they'd be interested in selling them. One local animal clinic accepted, and I put out a basket of treats that I would restock weekly. The clinic collected the money and generously let me keep 100 percent — I think they were helping me out because I was so young. I also sold my treats at local farmers markets and pet rescue fundraising events. At one of these events, I met a couple that was opening a doggie boutique, and they became my first wholesale customers. Getting my product into their store and developing a good relationship with them really helped get my business off the ground. New customers discovered my treats, and I was able to refer current customers and friends to that store for purchases.

As my business grew, I expanded my operations into using a rented commercial kitchen and subleasing retail space from one of my clients. I've used social media to its fullest and put out many posts to my friends encouraging them to try our new products. I've recently decided to stop working in a retail setting, but I still maintain multiple selling channels including: online sales, trade shows and events, and selling wholesale to retail outlets. I also created a fun "Biscuit of the Month" program — pet owners sign up for the service, and I mail them a pound-and-a-half of assorted gourmet treats every month. We also make custom cakes for doggie birthdays and other special occasions.

Working for myself has been a difficult but extremely gratifying and rewarding experience. I never could have foreseen the opportunities this venture would bring to me or anticipated meeting such an amazing group of mentors. I'm sure I would make more money in the short-term if I got a "regular" job, but in the end, I know it is going to pay off. I would not trade this experience for anything; I've gained so many valuable tools growing the business and received more recognition than I ever could have imagined. I also know that if I ever sell my business, I'll have enough to get me comfortably started in my next endeavor.

Words of Wisdom: Start small because this is a learning process. Everyone fails at some point, and you will make mistakes. If you never make a mistake, then you're probably not taking enough risk.

Previous chapters talked about using your artistic talents to make money through teaching, by commission, or while performing, but you also can create original pieces to sell at local craft fairs, flea markets, home décor stores, galleries, or online through your own website or artist-focused websites such as Etsy. *Chapter 4 went into detail about protecting your creations, setting your prices, and finding a market for your artwork. Refer back to the "Artistic Expression" section for tips and more information on the issues related to creating art for hire.*

Browse the categories listed on Etsy for ideas on the types of original art people are looking for. To make the most money, you'll have to tailor your artwork to appeal to a mainstream market and create pieces people want. For example, if you like to make wood carvings, work on small pieces that will fit on someone's mantle or coffee table. You won't be creating or selling masterpieces but using your artistic talents to make original pieces people will be proud to display, wear, or give as gifts. These will appeal to the widest customer base:

- Framed wall art made through: painting or drawings, calligraphy, or photography
- Pottery, ceramics, or glasswork
- Face painting or temporary tattoos
- Jewelry
- Hair, shoe, or backpack decorations
- Wood carving, wood burning, or wood art
- Yard artwork, such as gazing balls or seasonal flags
- Origami or paper-based art

Selling original art relies on getting your pieces in front of the people most likely to buy them. If you're painting abstract pieces, have a gallery showing or participate in some juried art shows. If you're making funky jewelry, set up booths at craft fairs or flea markets. The Internet also has made it easier to get exposure; hundreds of websites are available to showcase your artwork. As mentioned, Etsy is one of the best and easiest to use. To list your pieces on this website, you'll need to register for an account, then post pictures and descriptions for a small fee. You can link to Etsy through other social networking sites, and once buyers find you, they pay you directly, and you handle delivery. You can also sell through auctions sites such as eBay, online classifieds sites such as Craigslist, or set up your own website. Using the Internet to market your pieces will give you the broadest exposure possible and open the market beyond your geographic area.

▶ Handmade wares

People love to display unique handmade items. From soaps to baby booties, you can parlay your talents into a moneymaking venture and still tap into your creative side. You'll need some technical know-how and a workspace to create your wares. Good markets for these products include flea markets, craft fairs, or online sites such as Etsy. Browse through the categories on this website or search through your local craft fairs to get a feel for the products people buy and the price ranges of these items. Some popular categories to start out with include:

- Handmade wood furniture or home décor
- Soaps or lotions
- Candles
- Crocheted or knitted pieces
- Handmade paper or cards
- Hand-printed greeting cards or invitations
- Weavings, knitted pieces, or hand-embroidered furnishings

A Note about Sales Tax

In most parts of the United States, buyers must pay a sales or consumption tax on items they purchase. The tax is a set percentage of the total purchase price. Sometimes necessities such as food or clothing are exempt. The rules vary widely by city, county, and state, but in all cases, it is the seller's responsibility to collect the sales tax and send it on to the appropriate government agency. *Chapter 10 will cover this topic in detail.* Make sure you check the requirements before you start selling your products. You'll be responsible for paying the sales tax even if you don't collect it from your customers.

CHAPTER EIGHT

A Few Business Basics

After all these job listings, you probably have a nice list of potential business ideas, and you're ready to work. Before you jump right in, though, read the remaining chapters for more information on how to succeed in business. Of course, if all you're doing is mowing a few lawns, you don't need to become well educated in the world of finance. Making more money and enjoying the process, however, is more complicated than hauling the lawn mower out of the garage. If you approach your job with some basic knowledge and develop a minimal plan, you will make more money and have a better chance at success.

The following four chapters will walk you through the basics of business: handling customers, solving problems, and keeping your bank accounts in order. These chapters aren't meant to be an official, advanced guide to running a business, however. In fact, you could pick any one of the following segments and find a shelf full of books written on that one topic. What you can take away, though, is a beginner's understanding and a road map to seeking out more information. If you have questions, find a current book at your local library, or do an online search for more in-depth information. *Appendix B has listings for great business, marketing, and banking resource books and websites.*

Also, don't ignore the best resources available to you right now: your parents, your teachers, and other trusted adults in your life. Believe it or not, they know a lot about these topics and are more than willing to help you. Never be afraid to say, "I do not know," because that is where true learning begins. So, now onto the nuts-and-bolts of getting your business started.

Is It a Worthwhile Venture?

Before you commit your time or resources, you need to determine if your hard work will result in a profit. You could invest hundreds of dollars and dozens of hours to make only a few dollars. You might enjoy these hours, but one of the main benefits of working for yourself is making more money than working a regular job. After all, if you're going to put in the time, you should at least end up with something to show for it.

Setting your goals

Your first step for success is to set your business goals. This is not a lifetime commitment, and your job setup only might need to last until you graduate. Set small goals and review your list as your business grows. Now is a good time to talk with your parents, too, because they might have a different plan for some of the money you earn. Narrow down your goals by asking yourself these questions:

1. How much money do I want to make, what is the money for, and how much time do I have to make it? An example of a goal for working would be: "I need to make $1,500 during summer break to pay for my senior class trip."

2. Do I want to increase my skills or learn something new? Your work time can improve on what you know or gain you experience in the field. Working with a mentor can be a goal to set. Also, you can take on jobs that will challenge you to learn more.

3. Do I want to build a business or make a quick buck? Either goal is acceptable, and they aren't mutually exclusive, but the answer will affect how you approach your work. For instance, if you want to build a long-term business, you will need to nurture every customer for future sales.

4. How much time and effort do I have to put toward this job? Be brutally honest with yourself, and remember that your No. 1 job is to be a student and enjoy your high school or college years. Piling on too many jobs in an already loaded schedule not only will lead to work problems but also can affect your grades and personal life.

Do you have competition?

Even the best plan will run up against obstacles, and you need to understand your business to decide if you and your product have room in the marketplace. Start by reviewing the need for your product or service. For example, if you live in a high-rise apartment building, you probably won't find many customers for a dog-walking business. Tailor your offerings to find customers easily, or you'll be spending many non-billable hours looking for work. *Subsequent sections in this chapter will talk about finding customers.*

If you find a need for your product, others probably found the same need, and you will encounter competition. Depending on the uniqueness of your product or service, competition might not be an issue, but you most likely will be jockeying with others for the same customers. Assessing your competition doesn't have to be time-consuming or highly scientific — start by asking people you know if they've heard of anyone else offering a similar product. Skim through the ads in your local paper or look at the fliers hanging in the grocery store. If you find a lot of similar offerings, research a little more to find out exactly what they're selling and what their price range is. You can compete with anyone as long as you are dependable, offer quality service or products, and keep your prices within the average range.

You can also do more advanced market research, such as handing out surveys to potential customers or even hiring a marketing firm to perform demographic tests or market assessments. These will cost money and are designed to help more established, bigger businesses. They might be appropriate someday, but for now, your personal observations should be enough. Again, by starting small, you'll be able to determine the potential for success quickly. If you aren't finding customers or selling product, you'll know you need to adjust your work plan. If you're having trouble meeting orders because you are so swamped with customers, you'll know there's room for growth in your business. Don't let the big-business guys fool you; even corporate giants make decisions based on gut instinct. The key is to not invest too much time or money until you are familiar with the market.

Assessing the market climate can help you find areas in which your competition is lacking or missing opportunities. You can turn these missed chances into an advantage. For example, if you've browsed the farmers market and found people selling fruit and veggies but no fresh-cut flowers, you can set up your business to provide this product. Also, if your competition is having problems with service delivery or pricing, you can step in and provide a better option. There is usually room for one more business in the marketplace — you just need to discover the right niche that will appeal to customers.

Setting your prices

You'll have to pick a price range for your service or product, and this price is heavily dependent on where you live and how much competition you're facing. Each job listing gave you a going rate for the field, but there is a lot of room on either side of this number. You primarily must stay at or below the average rate for your area — as a teenager with minimal experience, people will expect you to charge at the lower end. The best way to set your prices  is to find out how much your competition charges. Make sure you are comparing similar services or products. Finally, factor in your production and overhead costs such as raw materials or shipping expenses because your final price must be more than what you have put into the venture. Retail stores charge at least double of what they pay for their products so they can cover the costs of their storefront, supplies, advertising, and staffing costs. These costs of doing business are considered "overhead" expenses. You will have less overhead expense than a retailer or larger business, so you can charge a lower price and still make money.

In some situations, the market will determine the price of your goods, such as when you are selling items through online auctions or if the product you are selling is in high demand. In these cases, you will need to know a general base value to set your minimum or reserve price. The best-case scenario is to have a bidding war for your item because this can drive the price up past your minimum — and it will keep going until bidders feel the item has reached its maximum value. Getting the buzz going about your product and building excitement with good marketing is a way to hike up these prices. *Tips on marketing will be discussed in a later section.*

In some cases, such as carpentry work or long-term babysitting jobs, the customer will ask you to bid on the job or provide an estimate of total costs. Your estimate should show all the costs associated with completing the job, including the materials and labor costs. Estimates also include a timeline of when each phase of the project will be done. As a beginner, it can be difficult to estimate your time and materials, so it is best to ask your parents or another adult to help you. As you get more experience, you will know what's required to get it done. If your customer accepts your bid, you'll be expected to finish the job for this price and within this time. Give yourself a little wiggle room by adding a few extra hours and dollars in case unexpected problems crop up. Check out the costhelper® website at **www.costhelper.com** for some estimating tools and lists, searchable by job title.

How will you get it all done?

When you're self-employed, you're responsible for making sure everything is in place so the job can be done properly. If you worked at a "regular" business, these logistical tasks would be relegated to separate departments, such as accounting or maintenance. When you are the boss or the only employee, you must make sure everything is taken care of. For example, if you're selling crafts online, your customers expect a quality product but also a quick answer to questions and proper packaging of the item. Make sure you have a reliable way to monitor your listings and that you have the necessary bubble wrap to pack your sales.

Each job listing in the previous chapters talked about the unique logistics required to accomplish that particular job. As a refresher, let's go over the main areas nearly every self-employed worker needs to think about.

1. Equipment and supplies. What do you need to get the job done? How will you pay for this equipment, and where will you purchase it? Of course, much of the equipment or supplies you need are already in your home or at your customer's house. If it's OK with your parents, you can use this to start out, but as your business grows, plan on paying for your own supplies or buying your own equipment.

2. Space and storage. Do you have a space to work? You probably have a spot set up already where you do your homework, and this can double as a mini-office. You will be more productive if you are able to have a dedicated space where you can file and store records or leave out work that is in progress. If your work involves equipment or product inventory, you'll also need a space to store everything when it is not in use. Your parents most likely will let you take over a corner of the basement, garage, or guest bedroom for storage needs. Consider, too, if you're going to need space to meet with clients, and if so, arrange to have access to a professional, quiet area. You also can offer to meet customers at their home or office.

3. On-the-job needs and transportation. Are you going to need uniforms, work clothes, or display tables? How will you acquire these items, and how will you get them back and forth to your worksite? You'll also need a way to transport your product to the market or to the delivery service.

4. Are there restrictions, regulations, licenses, or permits required for your work? These can take months to acquire, so give yourself

plenty of time to get things in order. *Chapter 10 goes into detail about licensure and permits.*

Think about every step needed to succeed at your job — don't forget the simple things such as good walking shoes or a reliable cell phone. Knowing the logistical needs of your business will help you determine how much overhead expenses you will have. Spend as little money as possible to start up, and ask your parents to help you. As you start making money, you can feed some of the profits back into the business to pay for supplies, marketing, or new equipment. After you've been working for a while, your profits should outweigh your up-front expenses and ongoing overhead costs.

Staying Safe on the Job

The importance of job safety cannot be stressed enough for you, your belongings, and your customers. Be aware that as a self-employed worker, no one else will be looking out for you. You alone are responsible for practicing safe work methods and protecting your own personal safety and the safety of those impacted by your job. The U.S. government has a strong framework of laws designed to protect young workers. Even as a self-employed person, these safety laws still cover you, and they should be used as a guideline in shaping your workday. As with most government regulations, dozens of separate documents explain the rules and restrictions related to youth employment. These documents can be found by visiting the Department of Labor website at **www.dol.gov**; click on the Youth & Labor link. Some industries such as mining, medical care, or door-to-door sales have heavy restrictions, hours-worked limitations, and age qualifications. Please check the site for safety rules before you start because your parents or customers could get in trouble if you're working in an area not allowed for your age.

Protecting your personal safety and belongings

Even with rules in place, there are plenty of hazards on the job, especially when you are working alone. If you're going to be alone with strangers, protect yourself from danger — all the lessons you learned in elementary school still apply here. Listen to your gut instincts, meet with people in public places, and if it feels wrong, run, and call 911. Sadly, many people scan Internet postings or classified ads in an effort to lure teens into unsafe situations. In most cases, you don't need to look to strangers for work opportunities; you can find plenty of jobs with people you know or those your parents are acquainted with. If you must work with strangers, be sure your parents know your general schedule and with whom you are meeting. If possible, have them nearby, keeping tabs on you.

TIP!

You're allowed to decline a job if you feel unsafe or uncomfortable with the people or situation. You're also allowed to check your customer's references — if they're offended that you're asking, they are probably not the right person to work for anyway.

Depending on the work you are doing, you might have safety issues related to working with potentially dangerous equipment or supplies. This situation especially applies to the labor-intensive fields such as farm work, house

246 The Teen's Ultimate Guide to Making Money When You Can't Get a Job

cleaning, and carpentry. You must understand how to use every piece of equipment you come in contact with — even if you aren't personally using it, you still could be injured. Always ask if you have questions, and wear the proper safety gear required for your job. Don't work if you are tired, bring along a jug of drinking water, and take frequent breaks.

The third area of personal safety to think about is protecting your private information, such as bank accounts, debit cards, or online financial information. If you are using the Internet to do business, this is especially important. Reputable sites that handle money will have the "https" designation before their Web address. Use secure passwords for these sites, and never give out your personal banking information or your Social Security number unless you have initiated the contact. Many times hackers or scammers will send you an email saying "This is your banking website; there is an issue with your account, and we need to confirm your account number. Please send us your number or Social Security information for verification." This type of solicitation is a scam — banks will never contact you in this way. Before you give any information out, double-check the site's address and have your mom or dad check it out too.

Additionally, you will need to take steps to protect your equipment or products while you're working. If you keep equipment at your job site or use a bike to go from job to job, it is important to bring a lock along. If you rely on saved computer files or mailing lists, be sure to back up your data every day. If you are out in a public selling situation, keep an eye on your products and cash. Thieves love to target garage sales or market tables where the sellers leave the products or money bag unattended.

Internet safety

Using the Internet to find work is common and sometimes the best and only way to connect with customers. It can also be a connection to scammers, hackers, and general bad guys. In addition to protecting your personal financial information, watch out for scams trying to trick you out of money or products. The best way to protect yourself is to work through reputable selling sites that offer tips for avoiding scams. They have seen it all and are happy to check out an offer for you if you are unsure. Secondly, work with sites that offer a seller and buyer review or feedback option and include secure payment arrangements such as PayPal or an escrow service such as on Elance. You pay a small fee for these protections, but it's worth it. A great consumer-focused website with information about Internet scams can be found at **www.lookstogoodtobetrue.com** — click on the "Teen Center" link for good articles about protecting yourself while online.

Protecting your customer's safety

In many personal care jobs, you will be entrusted with the complete well-being of your customer's home, children, pets, or personal belongings. There are inherent risks when caring for young children or vulnerable older people — make sure you can handle the requirements adequately to ensure a safe environment. You'll also be expected to protect your client's privacy and personal information including computer data or vacation plans. For example, if you've been hired to watch someone's home while they are on vacation, don't go on Facebook to tell everyone you are watering Mr. Jones' plants because he is out of town. Also, if you're hired to handle a private matter, such as caring for a sick relative or planning a surprise birthday party, you will need to keep what you learn to yourself. Your discretion and professionalism in these areas will earn you more work.

Finding customers

This is the do-or-die portion of making money. You have an office set up, all your products in place, and a fabulous advertising campaign, but you still must find the right customer. Begin by sketching out who you think your customer is. Start with the most obvious buyer or end-user. This should take only an hour or so of brainstorming. For example, if you'd like to provide in-home elder care, your customers will be adult children of older people still living in their homes or elderly neighbors living in your town. Refer back to the section about your job, and you'll find ideas for identifying potential customers and where you can find them. Once you've identified your target customer, develop a plan to reach them. That plan should begin with the cheapest method possible, which is usually word-of-mouth or referrals gained through your personal network.

Networking

You don't need to spend hundreds or even tens of dollars to connect with potential customers. Word-of-mouth will garner you plenty of work, and once you start working and doing a good job, you will get more referrals. This commonly is referred to as "networking," and with social media sites such as Facebook or Twitter®, networking has become crucial for finding work. Your network is anyone you or your parents know and can include: teachers, aunts, uncles, grandparents, fellow charity group members, former employers, your parents' friends, your grandparents' friends, your friends' parents, people at your church, and so on. When put to good use, this network can get the word out quickly and spread your message to a wide circle of people.

When putting your network to use, be specific about the work you're looking for. Post to your social networking site and put up fliers where you think your potential customers will see them. Go door-to-door in your neighborhood or register on a reputable website that caters to your line of work. The more you get the word out, the higher your chances of connecting with a potential customer. If you're really brave, you can try "cold calling." This technique refers to calling a potential customer without any kind of previous contact and asking them for work. You can use referrals from your network — otherwise known as name-dropping — to open up the phone call before you start selling yourself. You've probably been involved with cold call or door-to-door sales through school fund-raisers. This isn't any different, except now you're selling your own company. Cold calling can be a bit scary but well worth it when looking for work. Sometimes the answer will be no, but always end your cold call with a plan for future contact or a time to meet in person. *An example of a script for cold calling is included in Appendix A.*

Using the Internet to find work

From selling jewelry on Etsy to listing video games on Craigslist to marketing vintage china on Ebay, the Internet opens up your customer base to everyone in the world. Of course, using these sites requires a bit of know-how because you're also competing with every other seller in the world. Remember, too, that you will deal with issues such as writing up descriptions about your product, paying the listing fees, and packaging your product for shipment. These are easily acquired skills, but you'll have to spend some time in the beginning learning how to work with the website.

> ## TIP!
>
> Even a simple email account can be a great way to connect with customers. Be sure to pick a professional-sounding name for your website or email address and avoid offensive or cutesy names.

Dozens of good books at your local library will walk you through every issue related to selling online. You can also find thorough information by browsing through the individual website's "Help" link or "How To" section. The key to success with Internet selling is to keep your feedback as close to 100 percent as possible. This is accomplished through accurate product descriptions and superb customer service or satisfaction guarantees. Look at the sellers on Ebay that

have the best feedback, and emulate their listings and service guarantees. *Appendix B includes numerous online sites for finding work.*

CASE STUDY: ON THE JOB WITH LANE SUTTON

Occupation: Social media coaching
Age: Started his business at age 14
Lane@LaneSutton.com
www.LaneSutton.com; http://
twitter.com/LaneSutton

Lane Sutton. Photo Courtesy of Lane Sutton.

I started my own website at a young age and wrote a book review on KidCriticUSA.com. Someone I featured in the article asked me to help her with her social media presence online, and that is sort of how I got started. Now I work as a social media coach and help train other businesses in using social networks like Facebook or Twitter to reach their customers effectively. I also do public speaking about online privacy and the social media revolution, and I've given presentations at colleges, business conferences, corporate events, and schools. I've also been featured on media outlets such as *The Wall Street Journal*, Forbes.com, CNN.com, and *The Young Icons* TV show.

I continue to believe in the power of social media and only expect this area to grow in the coming years. In a real-time world, social media puts your business in front of a world audience, builds your brand awareness, and gives you a voice. Social networks are becoming more effective at marketing than TV, radio, phone, print, and reality advertising, and best of all... it's free.

Lane's Top Five Tips for Maximizing Social Media in Business

1. Provide relevant, useful content media that does not directly promote your company but focuses on the general industry. Offer a link and call-to-action to direct readers to your promotional website or blog once they're interested and see the value you offer.

2. Start a blog with either WordPress.com or Blogger.com to write helpful articles to use your product or service. Here, you can share product news, specials, promotions, and helpful hints.

3. Create a Facebook fan page and invite your current and past customers to join to stay updated on your business. Engage with your customers, encourage feedback, and ask questions.

4. Create an account on Twitter.com to send short "tweets" of mainly content for others to share and forward to their followers. This circulates your business name and account for exposure as people retweet you. Twitter is best for national or online businesses to gain new customers.

5. Warning: Do not share your own personal information such as your exact address, location sharing, or phone on the Internet or websites. Use a general contact form that can be sent to your own email address — if possible use an anonymous email hosting site such as gmail.com or emailmeform.com.

Advertising and marketing

Any message you put out about your company is considered marketing, and you can find plenty of free or low-cost avenues to market your product. The key is to start small and review your results before adding on more advertising. If you're getting plenty of business through free or low-cost advertising, stop there. The less you spend on marketing, the more money will be left in profits.

Advertising and marketing fall into four broad categories, and most ad campaigns include a collection of pieces from every category. A campaign is a unified effort of marketing materials designed to build brand awareness and make sales. You don't need a full-blown campaign, but try to create advertising with a consistent look and feel, and make sure your message is consistent across all platforms. Consider these elements as you develop your marketing:

1. Traditional advertising, including printed newspaper ads or fliers, billboards, brochures, or radio and television ads. The time and money needed to produce some of these options can be prohibitive to most self-employed workers and aren't necessary to pull in customers. A small, simple classified ad or flier posted in your grocery store is sufficient. Your computer's word processing program has templates, graphics, and type fonts to help you create your own folder quickly. Most small newspapers also will make a small ad for you at no additional charge.

2. Public relations and press releases. This type of marketing refers to "events" you create as a way to build buzz around your product or service. For example, if a charity in your area is hosting a fundraiser, you could donate some of your product to their silent auction. Be sure to include your name and contact information with the donation. After the auction is over, you can write up a simple press release highlighting your donation and details about your company. You might get a small article or even a picture put in your local paper, and it will cost you next to nothing.

3. Blogs or websites. Many online selling sites have a "review" or blog section where customers can comment on their purchases. Ask your

customers to give you favorable reviews whenever possible. Consider starting your own blog as a way to highlight your product and build buzz about your business. Looking over existing blogs and reviews is also a great way to assess your competition and find ways to improve your product.

4. Public appearances, demonstrations, or free samples. If your product lends itself to a demonstration, set up a table in a public area and start showing off. If you already have a table or booth set up at a market, offer free samples of your products. Whenever possible, work to upsell your product line to existing customers.

You should create most of this advertising yourself and don't have to spend a lot of money to put your marketing in place. Most word processing programs have templates for creating printed documents and Web-hosting sites offer a free Web-creation program. If you are buying a newspaper ad or getting a lot of copies made, the newspaper or printer sometimes will offer free or reduced-rate design services. Remember to be creative, be concise, and include your name, phone number or email, and details about what you are selling. *Refer to Appendix A for examples you can use as templates to create your own marketing pieces.*

Interviewing or customer contacts

Every time you meet with a potential customer, put on your best performance. Whether you are sitting down to a formal interview with the boss or meeting customers at craft fairs, people use these encounters to decide if they will hire you or buy your product. No one likes to go on interviews — not even seasoned experts like your Mom and Dad. It is unavoidable, though, and you might as well hone your people skills now because you will have many more interviews in your future. The key to nailing your interview is to be yourself, be as honest as possible, and smile. Your customer does want to hire you and just needs assurance you can be trusted to deliver on your promise. Bring these important documents along to your interview or have them ready to hand out to potential customers:

- Résumé. This will be short because you don't have a lot of work experience, but you can highlight your achievements in school or through community work. Include any special training or work experience you have gained through regular employment or volunteering. Triple-check your grammar and spelling, and have your parents review it when you're done. Your word processing program includes a résumé template and many additional examples can be found online. *Appendix A shows an example of a teen résumé.*

- References. These are adults willing to vouch for you — preferably, people you have worked for, but they also can be teachers, mentors, or neighbors. List the person's name, relationship to you, and phone number, but be sure to ask each of them ahead of time if it is OK. Your references also can include before-and-after pictures of your work, examples of finished pieces, or reviews from satisfied customers. Always ask for references or keep records of every job you finish, and keep them on file for future use.

- Information about your company. For sit-down interviews and personal meetings, be ready with a printed list of services you offer and the prices of everything — this is sometimes called a "leave-behind." You must know, by heart, all the details of how to do the job and be able to explain how you will meet the needs of the customer. For more informal customer contacts, have a few business cards with you because you never know when a business opportunity will pop up.

These documents can be prepared easily with any word processing program — most have a template to work from. You also can get a small quantity of business cards printed at large copy centers such as FedEx® or Staples®. *Examples of these documents are shown in Appendix A.*

Like it or not, when you're being interviewed, you're being examined. The first impression you make when you walk in the door will positively or negatively affect the interviewer's perception. A bad first impression could cost you the job. So, it's essential to be on time, dress appropriately, use your best manners, leave your cell phone and iPod in the car, and be friendly. Shake the person's hand — have your parents practice a good handshake with you. Look the other person in the eye, speak clearly, and don't be afraid to ask your own questions. Unless you are interviewing for a creative or progressive job such as an artist or musician, now is not the time to wear funky jewelry, over-the-top makeup, or extreme perfume.

During your interview, be prepared to explain exactly how you can help solve a problem. Give specifics on your product or services, how you will approach the job, and what guarantee you offer. If possible, give examples or tell stories of satisfied customers, especially if you have gotten the meeting through a mutual acquaintance. Be clear during the interview, too, with what you won't do or when you can't work. Avoid saying things such as "I need this job" or "You're really helping me out." They're looking to you for help in some way and want to know you can deliver.

As the interview winds down, you will have to "close the deal." This can be as simple as asking for an order, settling on a price, or setting up an appointment for further planning. It's not about winning but about finding a middle ground where you are satisfied with the deal and your customer is happy with what they have received. Be assertive and confident without being pushy, and make it easy for your customer to hire you. When the interview is over, be sure to shake hands again, say thank you, and make sure you leave behind your contact information. Better yet, follow up with a handwritten thank-you note and a free sample of your product.

Job Performance

Getting the job or selling the product is just the beginning. It's important to use good job skills to keep your customers happy. Unlike a regular job, you won't receive periodic formal reviews or pay raises. Your reviews and pay increases will come in the form of referrals, additional job offers, or more sales. The skills you needed to ace the interview should be carried over into your job performance:

- Stay focused while at work. No texting, no iPod games, and no meeting with friends. Give your customer all your attention while you are on the clock.

- Work hard. Don't slack off, especially when you're being paid by the hour. Look busy, even if you're not.

- Use good manners and act professionally. Watch your language and behavior, especially around young kids.

- Problem solving. Make sure your customer is satisfied; try to solve every problem; and follow-up afterwards.

- Add value. Look for opportunities to go the extra mile to make your product or service stand out.

TIP!

Develop a calendar system to keep track of your appointments. Most computer-based calendars can be programmed to give you reminders. If your customers hire you for irregular services, such as a twice-a-year garage cleaning, schedule a reminder so you will remember to call them ahead of time to set up your next job.

CHAPTER NINE

A Few Money Basics

Once you start making money, you'll need a way to track it, save it, and use it to grow your business. From buying work equipment to filling the tank with gas to keeping a well-stocked inventory, you're going to need to find a way to pay for your business expenses. Spend as little as possible at first in case your idea doesn't pan out. Even better, look for ways to barter or exchange services with others as you get started.

Overall, the best approach to funding your startup is to avoid debt if possible. Taking out a small loan from the Bank of Mom and Dad is acceptable, but try to stay away from using true bank loans or credit cards. These routes will cost you service fees and interest charges, which will eat into your profits. Once you start making money, you can pay your parents back and put some money aside to pay for future costs. Your goal from the beginning should be to make as much profit as possible.

Where to Keep Your Money

You might not believe this now, but eventually you will have too much money to stuff into your piggy bank. If you are using the Internet to sell or working with multiple suppliers, you'll also need a cash-free way to conduct business. You have many options for stashing your money, and this chapter will give you the basics of banking and give you the tools to start thinking about money. Research this topic further at your local library or visit many of the finance-oriented sites available online. The more you know, the faster your money will grow. A great book to start with is *A Complete Guide to Personal Finance: For Teenagers and College Students*, also by Atlantic Publishing. For now, let's get a brief look at your options in banking and running your business.

If you're under 18 years old, your bank will require you to open your account with a parent. Your parent will have access to the money and to your account statements. For new accounts, you will need to provide identification such as your student I.D. card, your Social Security number, and your permit or driver's license. Bring these with you to open your bank account. If you're opening multiple accounts, keep them at the same bank, because it'll be easier to access your money and monitor your account activity.

Checking or debit accounts

If your work requires buying supplies or paying for deliveries, your best option would be to open a checking account. This is an efficient way to manage your money and is much easier than carrying around wads of cash. A check can be sent securely through the mail to distant suppliers, you will have a written record of all your transactions, and if your account comes with a debit card, you'll have ready access to cash money. Most checking accounts have fees, though, so be sure to shop around for the best deal. Your bank might also offer a "student checking account" with reduced fees and requirements. You probably won't be writing that many checks or depositing large amounts of money, so look for an account that doesn't require a minimum balance or monthly activity level.

When a vendor cashes your check, the money is taken out of your account, so make sure to record each check and keep a running total of your balance. This list of recorded checks and deposits into your account is called a check register. Here is an example of what your check register might look like:

Check #	Date	Transaction Description	Withdrawal	Deposit	Balance
	11/23	ATM Withdrawal	$20.00		$453.22
112	11/23	Galore Bookstore	$12.68		$440.54
	11/26	A-OK Gas Station	$22.97		$417.57
	11/26	Paycheck		$400.00	$817.57
113	11/28	Car Payment	$194.25		$623.32
	11/28	Phones & More Outlet	$14.99		$608.33

If you write checks and don't have enough money in your account, your check will "bounce," and you will be charged an overdraft or "insufficient funds" fee from the bank and sometimes a fee from the person cashing the check. These fees can range from $10 to $50 per check. Some banks offer overdraft protection in which they will pay the check even if you do not have enough money in your account. This protection will cost you a per-check fee and usually has a maximum daily limit.

Depositing money in your checking account can be done at the bank window, electronically from another account, from an online payment site, or through the mail. If you're depositing a check you've received, you will need to endorse the check by signing it on the back. Wait until you are at the bank before you sign the check because a signed check can be cashed by anyone. If you're sending the check through the mail, write "FOR DEPOSIT ONLY" under your endorsement. Familiarize yourself with your bank's deposit policy because banks often will hold a deposited check for a few days before making the money available to you. This is to protect the bank in case the check you've deposited doesn't clear its bank.

At the end of each month, you'll receive a bank statement showing all the activity on your account during the past 30 days. Use this statement to "balance" your checkbook. This process helps you find missed checks or withdrawals and helps you identify accounting errors. To balance your checkbook, go through each line item on the statement and compare it to your check register. At the end, you'll compare your balance to the bank's balance, and they should match. This entire process does seem complicated, but it is easy to manage once you have done it. Ask your parents to help you the first time.

Most checking accounts also come with an ATM or debit card. A debit card functions as a check because the money is automatically deducted from your account. It can be used like a credit card for making electronic or online purchases or for withdrawing money when you are traveling or the banks are closed. Debit cards often carry usage fees, so be aware of the costs before you start using your card a lot. Also, make sure to record these withdrawals in your check register. Be careful with your card because if it is stolen and used, money will be withdrawn until you discover the theft and cancel your card. Your bank most likely will refund you the money eventually, but it will take a lot of time and hassle. For that reason, it is important to set secure PIN codes on your card.

What is a PIN?

Your debit account will require a special code called a personal identification number or PIN. It is a series of numbers you will need to enter to use your debit card. Protect this code, do not write it on your card or keep it in your wallet, do not tell others, and choose a number that isn't easy to guess — avoid using your birthday or phone number. If someone has your PIN and debit card, they will have complete access to your account and your money.

Prepaid Debit Card

A prepaid debit card functions much like a gift card but can be used anywhere. For a small fee, you can purchase these cards in any denomination at most banks or credit unions. They are used wherever credit or debit cards are accepted but are less secure because they don't have PINs or other protections such as signature requirements. They are, however, an excellent way to shop online because once the dollar amount is reached, no more money can be spent.

Savings accounts

A savings account is the simplest investment account offered by your bank. You keep your money in the account but have access to the cash whenever you need it. The bank pays you a small fee or "interest" on your balance. This interest is quite low, in the 1- to 3-percent range depending on the amount you have deposited. This interest accumulates over time, is added to your balance, and then earns more interest — this is called compound interest. You won't get rich off your interest earnings, but a savings account is a great place to let your money sit until you need to use it and is much safer than stashing your money in a shoebox.

The Federal Deposit Insurance Corporation (FDIC) protects money deposited in United States banks with some restrictions. If your bank is robbed, if it burns down, or if it goes out of business, you'll still be able to get your money through the FDIC system. Look for the FDIC sticker at your bank or visit the website at **www.fdic.gov** to learn more about this program.

Most banks offer a basic student or youth savings account that will not have fees or restrictions. This is a great place to start out, and as you learn more about banking and accumulate more money, you can branch out into more complicated, higher-earning investment accounts. *These options will be covered at the end of this chapter.* Once you open your savings account, you can deposit money as often as you wish and withdraw money whenever you need it. Banks will allow access to your savings account electronically, so you can transfer money to other accounts as needed. Some banks might require a minimum balance, so shop around for the best deal. You will receive a monthly or quarterly statement from your bank regarding your savings account activity. Review this, too, to make sure everything has been accurately recorded.

TIP!

Want to see how fast your money can grow? Visit this website from the Council for Economic Education, **www.econedlink.org**, for some fun, interactive savings calculators and graphs.

Personal bank loans

With good credit, you can secure a loan for anything including business equipment, a car, a boat, a house, or operating expenses for business startups. Of course, this money doesn't come cheaply. The bank charges fees for establishing the loan and then charges interest for the life of the loan. The interest compounds in the same way it does with a savings account, except this time you're paying the bank over and above what you've borrowed.

As an example, you take out a car loan of $5,000, at an interest rate of 8 percent, with a 24-month repayment period. Each month you'll pay the bank a payment of $226.14. By the end of the loan period, you'll have paid a total of $5,427.36 or an additional $427.36 more than the loan amount.

Loan rates vary widely according to your creditworthiness, the purpose of the loan, and the length of time needed to pay it back. Sometimes you will be asked to "put up collateral" toward the loan. This means you're guaranteeing your payment with another piece of property such as a car, a boat, or an expensive piece of jewelry. If you don't pay the loan back, the bank can seize the property you have put up for collateral. As a young person with no credit history or collateral, you'll find it difficult to secure a bank loan. In some cases, a bank will lend you money if you have another adult as a cosigner. A cosigner is responsible for paying the loan if you don't make payments and must pass a credit check or put up collateral, also. With these points in mind, you can see why getting a bank loan should be your last resort for money — and please, talk with your parents about the issues related to taking out a personal loan.

Credit cards

Credit cards are glorified bank loans that carry even higher interest rates than a personal loan — sometimes as high as 25 percent. If you charge something that costs $100 and don't pay off your balance right away, you will owe the credit card company $125 dollars, and they'll continue to charge interest on this balance until you pay it off. Unlike regular bank loans, credit card companies willingly give accounts to those with poor credit histories, and they love to target young adults. Once you turn 18, you will start getting credit card offers. Be wary of these first offers, as they usually carry high interest rates and hidden fees, such as maintenance charges or fees for exceeding your credit limit.

Credit cards companies are in the business to make money; this is the only reason they're offering you credit. It's easy to build up debt that will take years to pay off. If you miss a payment, your credit history will be affected, and the credit card company can assess you exorbitant fees and raise your overall interest rate. As you get older and apply for a job or try to buy a house, a bad credit history could make it difficult to accomplish these goals.

Credit cards, though, do have some use in the world of business. They are more secure and protected than a checking account and safer than cash. If someone steals your card and charges something, the credit card company will handle the dispute quickly, and you won't be out any money. If you buy something and it arrives broken or different than described, you can use the buyer's protection insurance included with most credit cards. You'll also receive a statement every month with your purchases clearly outlined. Many cards, too, offer perks such as travel miles or dividend checks after a certain amount of purchases.

How to select your first credit card

If you feel your business needs a credit card, selecting the right card should be approached as one more business decision. Don't be swayed by flashy offers of "introductory rates" or free gifts. Shop around for the best deal and choose a credit company that fits your long-term plan and your business needs. Read the fine print of each offer so you're aware of fees, rates, and potential penalties. Look for a card with a low interest rate, no annual fee, and premiums such as air miles — these cards might be hard to secure with your limited credit history but are worth searching for. Visit the website **www.bankrate.org** for a good comparison tool of current credit card offers. If you're a member of a credit union, special club, or society or you have an established banking relationship, start your search with these outlets because you might be able to secure a better deal.

No matter what type of card you choose, you must be disciplined to use a credit card, and the key is always to pay off your balance each month. You won't be charged interest during this time, and you can use this activity to build up your credit history. Once you have built up a successful credit history, you will be able to secure credit cards and loans with more favorable rates. If you're going to use a credit card for your business, keep a separate savings account in which you deposit the money each month that you then will use to pay off your balance. For some great tips and ideas for using credit cards, visit the Federal Reserve website at **www.federalreserve.gov/consumerinfo**.

TIP!

If you are concerned about piling on debt too fast, try starting out with a card with a low credit or spending limit of $500. You'll still be charged interest on this balance until you pay it off, but the low limit will keep you from going overboard.

Online banking

With the convenience of online banking, you can manage your business from any location, and these services make it possible to work with customers all over the world. You keep track of all your accounts by logging on, and you'll have a handy electronic record of all your banking activities, which will make completing your accounting chores fast and straightforward. Just make sure to use a secure connection protected from hackers, use high quality passwords, and carefully guard these passwords. This type of banking functions much like a regular checking or savings account and can be divided into a few entities:

1. Online banking services from a bricks-and-mortar bank. These are additional or supplemental services offered to the bank's customers through an online website. Services include access to account information, online applications for loans, funds transfer, and general customer service. Some banks charge extra for accessing your account electronically, so check the fees before you use the online bank office.

2. Online payment services. These services, such as PayPal, allow you to invoice customers, receive and track payments, resolve disputes, and electronically transfer money to your regular bank account. You will be charged a fee for every function you use, so factor these fees into your overhead costs. These sites are highly encrypted, and the service protects the customer's credit card number so payments can be sent and received without revealing account information to either party. Research the individual site for more information, and be sure to use a site that begins with https.

3. Online investment services. You can choose anything from a basic savings account to a high-risk stock portfolio. These sites, too, offer

a multitude of investment information and research tools, and they are great places for the beginner to learn more about the world of investing. They will charge fees for services. Choose a reputable service such as Ameritrade®, E*TRADE®, or Scottrade®, choose a high quality password, and select a site beginning with https. *Information on investing is including later in this chapter.*

Depending on your business, online banking might be your best option for billing, collecting, and saving money. Research your options thoroughly and make sure to select a service that is secure and established and that has low service fees. Your hometown bank will offer the most personal service, but online banking will expand your network beyond your immediate neighborhood. Consider a combination of local and online banking accounts to meet your business needs.

Managing Your Money

As your funds start to build, you will need to keep track of everything that is coming in and going out. Stashing money into one bank account is a great way to save up, but it might not be the best strategy for running your business efficiently. You will need to review your moneymaking goals and assess the financial requirements of keeping your business running. For example, do you need a certain amount of money each month to pay for cookie-making supplies? If so, you'll need to set this amount aside in an easily accessible account. Having your money readily available is referred to as "liquidity."

How to bill or collect payment

Most customers will pay you on the spot for your product or as soon as you have completed the job. However, in some cases, for example when you are hired for a long-term assignment, you will need to discuss the payment plan before you start working. Some customers will pay you at the end of the week, while others will want to pay you each day. Whatever arrangement works for you is fine as long as you discuss it ahead of time.

The best way to keep your accounts in order is to create an invoice or bill to give your customer when the work is done. An invoice makes your business more official, provides a written trail for you and your customer to refer to, and gives you a way to track your work over time. The invoice should state what work was done, what the per-unit or per-hour rate was, and how much is owed. Be sure to include your contact information on the invoice so your customer can send your payment. Depending on the type of work you are doing, the jobs can be invoiced individually as a one-time product sale or on a monthly basis such as ongoing lawn care. Be sure your invoice states that payment is due upon receipt and spell out the payment methods you prefer. Most word processing programs offer a simple invoice template, and office supply stores sell receipt books perfect for writing out invoices. *Appendix A includes a sample invoice to use as a template.* Most online billing sites offer invoicing services with which you can create invoices and billing statements to send electronically.

TIP!

Be sure to file copies of each invoice, and mark them "paid" as you receive payment.

If you are selling things online, use a payment service such as PayPal, and make sure the payment clears your bank before you ship the item. State clearly in your listings that you only accept payment through these arrangements and will not ship the item until the payment has cleared. Larger sites such as eBay have feedback ratings for buyers, too, and you can leave negative feedback if the sale does not go well. If you are selling through classifieds or face-to-face, avoid taking personal checks unless you know the person writing the check. Cash is the best currency, but avoid taking large bills such as $50 or $100 bills, as they frequently are counterfeited.

Sadly, once and a while a customer will try to get out of paying. Your first step should be to make sure the customer is satisfied with your work. If not, do what you can to make it right, but do not expect to be paid extra. If they are just trying to avoid payment, you don't have a lot of recourse, besides enlisting your parents' help with collection. Be sure to cross these customers off your list because they probably will try to skip payment again.

Keeping good financial records

Tracking finances is probably not going to be your favorite task, but it is necessary to keep things running smoothly and to ensure your money is used wisely. After a few months, you will be able to review your expenses and find ways to save money. You also can use your spreadsheets to keep records of customers. Your goal is track where the money comes in and how it is spent, and leftovers are yours to keep. This recordkeeping can be as simple as an old-fashioned, handwritten line item ledger book or as high-tech as an Excel spreadsheet. Choose whatever method works for you, and make recording information part of your routine.

> **TIP!**
>
> Computerized records such as those used in the program QuickBooks®
> are easy to search and organize by category. The computer will do the
> column calculations automatically — a handwritten ledger will have
> to be tallied by hand. Ask your parents about the system they use, and
> try it out for a month to see if it will work for you.

Business accounting can become complex when it includes tracking
amortization, depreciation, operating costs, employee expenses, and so on.
More information on upper-level accounting can be found at your library or
through talking with your school's accounting teacher. For large businesses,
this information is essential for growth or investor development. For your
small business purposes, though, a simple system of tracking money in and
money out will do fine. Be sure to include everything — even the cost of
repairing a flat bike tire or filling up the gas tank. At your level of business,
recordkeeping can be simple and should include these two items:

- Income or accounts receivable. Your record should include columns
  for the amount, date of receipt, item description, and name of the
  buyer if possible. Include all purchases including debit cards, online
  banking, and any associated fees.

- Expenses or accounts payable. This can be a separate ledger or
  combined with the income sheet. Again, include columns for date,
  amount, item description, and to whom the payment was made.
  Be sure to flag recurring expenses and enter the due dates on
  your calendar.

Revenue or income is all the money that comes into your account through
sales or investments. Business expenses are paid from your revenue. Profit
is the money left after expenses are paid. If your expenses are higher than
your income, you will be losing money. A profit margin refers to the room

or amount between your income and expenses. If you take in $500 per month and have $250 in expenses, your profit margin is $250. You can also use this margin to calculate your true hourly rate, if that matters to you. If it took you 25 hours to earn the $500 in revenue, you made $10 per hour.

If you have opened a checking account, your bank statement or check register should have all the information you need to track your income and expenditures. Keep a running tally of your money because you will be able to plan ahead and find ways to improve your operations. If you find that it is difficult to track your daily spending, try carrying a small notebook with you to enter data as you spend or earn.

Setting a budget

Sometimes you have to spend money to make money, and if you are going to have a future expense, you will need to plan ahead. A budget is simple to put together, and your business budget and personal budget can be put together in the same document. If you're planning to use money earned through allowance or gifts to run your business, include it in your income. If you're planning to use business profits to pay for personal expenses, include them in your expenses column.

Most people set up their budgets on a monthly basis because many bills come due every month. Review your moneymaking goals, too, when determining your budget line items. Make your budget as complex or simple as you would like. The purpose of your budget is to provide you with a plan for funding your business, meeting your financial goals, and keeping everything running smoothly. Without a budget, bills can fall through the cracks, and it becomes hard to know where your money is going.

Budget Example

Let's consider a sample budget for Dave's "No More Ds" Tutoring Service:

After tracking his income and expenses for the last month, Dave can see how much money it takes to maintain his current level of clients and income. He sets up his budget using a simple word processing program and then transfers any important due dates to his calendar. This is what next month's budget looks like:

Income	
Description	**Projected Monthly Income**
Tutoring Jimmy Smith, 4x per month @ $20/session	80.00
Tutoring Janie Alberts, 8x per month @ $15/session	120.00
Tutoring Alan James, 4x per month @ $20/session	80.00
Study Group meeting, 2x per month at $10/per student x 3 students	60.00
TOTAL	**340.00**

Expenses		
Description	**Recurring expense/ due date?**	**Amount**
Gas for meetings	yes/as needed	20.00/month
Study group rental space	yes/1st of the month	50.00/month
Projected income tax	no/April 15	30.00/month
Paper, pencils, supplies	no/as needed	10.00/month
	TOTAL	**110.00/month**

With this budget outline, Dave can see that he should have $230 left over after his expenses are met. He then can allocate this money to meeting his goals, funding his upcoming business expenses, and taking a little profit for entertainment or personal purchases. If Dave's spending and saving goals exceed $230 per month, he'll have to find ways to streamline his expenses or make more money. Remember these are only projections, and at the end of the month, Dave should compare his projections to his actual revenue and expenses.

Some months might show little or no profit. This is especially true when you are first starting out and have many up-front costs. Most businesses review their profits or losses every three months (quarterly) and then yearly — this gives a better overall picture of average profits and helps when developing long-term projections.

Deciding how to spend your money is, of course, personal, but it is a good idea to put away at least 10 percent to cover unexpected business expenses. Without an emergency fund, you might have to shut down your business if something happens you cannot afford to fix. Consider, too, donating a small percentage to a local charity or your place of worship. Money or your valued product or service given to charity is tax-deductible, and you will feel good giving back to your community. You'll also get free business exposure through your donations. It is also OK to spend money on yourself — after all, that is one reason for working. Just make sure your personal expenditures fit within your overall savings goal.

With both good money tracking and a well-thought-out budget, you have the tools you need to run your business at maximum profit levels. Set up a review of accounts every few months and look over the areas eating into your profits. Are you spending too much on raw materials or supplies? Do you need to add customers or find ways to become more efficient? Are some of your products or services not paying off? After six months or so, look for trends in your operating costs or income levels to see if your expenses or workload fluctuates with the seasons. If you see a trend such as increased preseason supply costs, research times when these supplies go on sale, so you can stock up when they are at their cheapest price.

How to Save or Invest your Money

As mentioned previously, saving money is not limited to a low-interest savings account. Your choices depend on your savings goals and the amount of risk you are comfortable with. The highest paying investments also carry the highest risk for losing money. Choosing a selection of investments with varying degrees of risk allows you to keep some of your money ultra-safe while other chunks earn good returns. This is called "diversification" or developing a "portfolio" of investments. It is OK to dabble in the stock market, but be careful of dumping all your money into something you don't fully understand.

Keep in mind that entire industries are built around professionals and companies that only research and rate investments. They have an arsenal of tools and education for selecting potential investments — and yet they still often lose enormous amounts of money. As a beginner with little time or experience, you may find it difficult to choose the right investments. Even your parents use a money manager or stockbroker to help them manage their savings. This section is meant to give you a primer on your options in the hope that you will educate yourself more thoroughly or seek out an investment professional to help you. One of the best places to go to learn more is The Motley Fool (**www.fool.com/teens/teens03.htm**) designed for teens. Here you will find easy-to-understand explanations of every type of investment available on the market. It's also a great site for general money managing advice.

Setting a savings goal

Throughout this book, you have been asked to consider your goals for making money, and one of those goals is to save some money for college, a car, or even your first home. If you're planning to develop your job into a business, then saving toward growing your company also can be a savings goal. The amounts you need to save depend on your anticipated needs and the possibility of earnings or income. Set realistic goals for yourself, or it will seem impossible to succeed. Goals fall into two categories:

- Short-term savings. This is money saved to meet upcoming or immediate needs, such as an expected tax bill or kept as an emergency fund. These savings need to be liquid so you can access the funds whenever you need.

- Long-term savings. This is money put aside for far off, future needs such as college — you can only estimate how much you will need.

The difference between short-term versus long-term savings matters because it will affect the type of investment vehicles you select. Short-term savings should be kept in an easily accessed fund such as a savings account, and these accounts earn the lowest interest rate. Long-term money does not need to be accessed immediately and can be locked up in funds that require a certain amount of time for deposit, such as certificate of deposit. Longer deposit periods pay higher returns, but you'll pay penalties if you have to withdraw your money before the period is up.

CASE STUDY: ON THE JOB WITH GRACE HATTON

Occupation: Writer, editor-in-chief, and CEO of Moxie International LLC
Age: Started her business at age 16
info@gracehatton.com
www.gracehatton.com and www. missmoxieonline.com

Grace Hatton. Photo courtesy of Grace Hatton.

I grew up knowing I wanted to find something that could be my life's work. I have been writing since the age of 12, and so I began trying to get my work published. At the age of 16, my self-help book, *The Guys, The Roses, and The Regrets*, was published, and it became a best seller. After that, I created my own magazine, *Miss Moxie*, because I noticed how few teen magazines promoted beauty on the inside as well as the outside. I wanted to create a magazine that would show young women how to develop strong character and make a positive difference in the world.

I didn't have much money to fund my startup, so I promoted my magazines through social media, and this network remains a huge part of our marketing program. We've also formed strategic alliances with other women's companies and make additional money through selling magazine ads and subscriptions.

Besides being able to do what I love, I think one of the main benefits of working for yourself is freedom. I have total freedom to choose when I work, where I work, and what projects I want to work on. I can work as hard as I want and build my own destiny — of course, sometimes that means compromises in other parts of my life. My friends often tell me I work too much, but I honestly feel the pros outweigh the cons. I know, too, that I'm earning a lot more money now than if I was working at a regular job.

When it comes to money, I'm pretty disciplined, and I use the "jar system" to divide my funds. Here is how this works for me:

- 40% goes toward necessities
- 10% toward giving
- 10% toward financial freedom
- 10% toward education
- 10% toward long-term savings
- 10% toward play

This system allows me to organize my hard-earned money. I have found it is easy to become excited when you first start earning your own money, and without a plan, it will quickly disappear. Now, I stick to my plan, and I'm able to use my money to reach my goals and still have a little left over for fun.

Words of Wisdom: You can't run a successful business if you aren't passionate about what you are doing. So, find out what you love, and then figure out how you can build a business around it.

Types of investments

So, where do you put all that money? Check your goals, review your business plan, and get ready to start shuffling dollars. Remember, if it sounds too good to be true, it probably is. Avoid at all costs the offers in which you get a chance at a "fabulous, no-lose stock guaranteed to double over the next year." This offer does come with a guarantee — the guarantee that you will lose your money. Slow and steady does win the race in investing, and as a young investor, you have time on your side.

When it comes to selecting an investment, the lower the risk level, the lower the potential return. On the flip side, this means that high-risk investments also carry with them the potential of high returns. A well-diversified portfolio with a good combination of low- and high-risk stocks is the best plan for growing your money. The following sections will give you a simplified, basic explanation of investment options. You are strongly encouraged to research each option further before investing.

Savings account, certificate of deposit, or government savings bond: low risk, low return

As mentioned, a savings account has the lowest risk possible and gives you the best access to your savings. Also low risk but with more restrictions are the certificate of deposit (CD) or the savings bond. In both cases, you "purchase" the CD or bond at a fixed rate, and you cannot "sell" it back to the bank or government until a specified amount of time has passed. This time can range from one year to ten years or more. You are loaning your money to the bank or bond-issuer, and they do not have to pay you back until the loan term has ended. In exchange for leaving your money longer, you receive interest higher than a regular savings account.

Stocks: medium to high risk, low to high return

Stocks are shares of a company sold to the public through the stock exchange. Large companies need cash to operate, and by selling shares on the open market, they can raise these funds and grow their business. Stock prices range from pennies to thousands of dollars, and not all companies are publicly traded. The "stock market" or "Wall Street" is often referred to as the home of all this trading. Each day the activity of the stock market is tracked and as a whole will be considered "up" or "down." When investing in a stock, it is best to let it sit and not panic if the price goes up or down — it is only a loss if you sell your stock at a price lower than you paid for it. If you don't sell it, you only are losing money temporarily on paper.

You can buy or sell stocks through a stockbroker or investment banker, or you can do it yourself through websites such as Ameritrade. These websites offer some great investing trackers and are a great place to do research. Most brokers and trading sites charge a fee for either buying or selling, but they usually charge per transaction, not the amount of shares you're trading.

Exchange-traded funds, mutual funds, or index funds: medium risk, medium return

These funds are a combination of stocks linked together under one name and sold by brokerage firms. The selected stocks can range from the top ten producers to stocks considered organic. Your options in selecting a fund are endless, but watch for fees to invest in this manner. Many innocent-looking funds have hidden fees, especially when you try to sell or cash out. Some of these funds also have requirements and/or penalties regarding early withdrawal: IRAs, Roth IRAs, or 529 College Plans. Be careful as you select the fund, and read all the fine print regarding restrictions.

Other investing options: high risk, potentially high return

You don't necessarily have to put your money in a financial vehicle to make it grow. You can choose to buy real estate, precious metals such as gold or silver, or antiques and other collectibles. You even could loan your money to others and charge them interest. These options carry a high amount of risk and require an advanced knowledge in the particular investment area.

Tax implications and recordkeeping

All of these options carry tax implications such as paying long-term gains when you sell your stocks or taking a loss if an investment goes bad. Each investment account you own will send you a quarterly statement showing the account's activity, gains or losses, and any fees charged to you. At the end of the year, you might receive a tax form from your brokerage firm with important information regarding your accounts. It is important to keep thorough records, file these documents with your tax return, and make sure your tax preparer is aware of your overall investment portfolio.

A note about savings and college financial aid

If you have started planning for college or are already in college, you have heard of the Free Application for Federal Student Aid (FAFSA.) Any college student seeking financial aid based on need must fill this form out yearly. Your income and assets and your parents' income and assets will be recorded on this form and calculated into your "Expected Family Contribution."

Some assets are exempt; only a small percentage of your or your parents' net worth is used — the government doesn't expect you to contribute every single cent you have toward college.

If you do have a substantial amount of money put away in savings, your needs-based financial aid could be affected. However, having a chunk of money in the bank will give you more options, and you won't have to worry about selecting your school based on cost. Remember that many scholarships and financial aid awards are based on academics or community involvement, so you still will have options for finding college money. Most colleges now offer a FAFSA calculator on their websites so you can get a good estimate of where you stand with financial aid. You also can ask your school counselor to help you determine how much you can expect to receive.

Learn more, and talk with mom and dad

This chapter has been a starting point for you to start your journey into the world of finance. Before you make any major investment decisions, talk with your parents or another trusted adult. They can give you good advice and help you weigh your options. Educate yourself as much as possible before you put money into something, and do not be afraid to talk with an expert or professional. *Look through Appendix B for listings of great investment books and websites.* Remember to start small until you are comfortable with what you are doing.

CHAPTER TEN

Beyond the Basics

Running a small business or working for yourself requires some business skill and administrative duties. A well-run, efficient business allows you to spend most of your work-time in billable activities and less time on non-billable administrative chores. The previous chapters covered most of what you need to know to get started and maintain a small mini-business. This chapter will cover the more involved issues you'll run into as you grow your business, add customers, and even take on employees. Most of these areas are optional and will not apply to your situation. There is no set order to accomplishing these tasks — some people prefer to write their business plans first, while others set up their business structures. As your business develops, you'll know which steps you need to grow.

The first two segments of this chapter, Taxes and Liability, are required reading. These issues affect you no matter what type of work you are doing or how many hours you put in. If you earn money, you must file taxes. If you sell a product or service, you might also need to pay sales tax to your city, county, or state. If you are handling products, people, or equipment, you will need to understand your liability risks. Do not skip these sections, as making a mistake with taxes or insurance coverage can cost you a lot of time and money.

The remaining sections will cover more complex issues, and it might feel a bit like sitting in econ class. Some people find these nitty-gritty business details interesting while others dread even thinking about it. If you fall into the latter category, this chapter might be painful for you, but you must get through it if you're serious about running your own business. So, get yourself a latte or cold soda, and wade through until you have a basic understanding of the concepts.

An A+ Online Business Guide: the United States Small Business Administration or SBA

Every issue in this chapter is explained on the SBA's website (**www.sba.gov**). The website is easy to navigate with numerous links, templates, and even chat rooms moderated by successful businesspeople. Your taxes pay for this tool, so put it to good use.

This chapter will provide you with a beginner's understanding. It is highly recommended that you seek more detailed information or find a professional to help you. Look for someone with experience helping small business owners who can handle more than one area of assistance, as this will save you money in consulting fees and appointment times.

Taxes

Taxes are monies collected by every level of government to pay for services they provide, such as schools, roads, and other public services. People pay taxes on everything from property to retail purchases. Most of these taxes are built into the final price you pay, so you might not realize you're paying a tax. When you start earning money, you will need to report your income and file an income tax form every year. The government then collects a percentage of this income as taxes — numerous deductions, income limits, and other restrictions limit the amount you're required to pay.

Income tax

When you work at a regular job, your employer deducts payroll taxes from your wages before issuing your paycheck. These taxes are divided into Social Security tax, federal or state withholding, and Medicare tax, and your employer sends the money to the appropriate government agency. At the end of the year, you will receive a W-2 form with the total tax deductions shown. This form then is used to fill out your income tax form, which must be filed on or before April 15. This form allows you to enter deductions such as school, business, or health expenses, which will reduce the amount of income

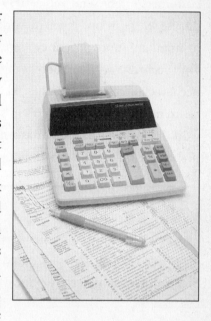

you are taxed on. In most cases, young people end up getting a tax refund because they do not make enough to require a tax payment. Yes, you can get money back from the government!

When you are a self-employed person, no one is going to send you a W-2 or deduct taxes from your paycheck. You, however, still will be required to file taxes and pay regular income tax and self-employment Social Security tax. If you don't make the payment, you will be fined, so it is wise to set aside a portion of your earnings as the year goes on even if you don't think you will owe money. A good rule of thumb is to assume you will owe 10 to 20 percent of your total income. If you have a profitable year, it could be more than 20 percent. Once you get to that level of taxes, you'll probably start paying estimated taxes every three months. Your accountant can help you determine if quarterly filing will work better for you.

If you're working as an independent contractor or consultant, your customers might send you a 1099-Form showing how much they paid you during the year, but if you're working for a lot of different people or taking in small amounts of money, you won't have forms for all of your income. Your records and checkbook will be the only evidence of income. You will need to claim all your income, whether you receive a form or not. You might be exempt from income taxes in some circumstances such as when you are working for your parents or as a household employee. Check with your tax preparer for more information regarding these situations.

TIP!

If you hire employees, you might be required to collect payroll taxes or issue them a 1099 at the end of the year. Be sure to check with your accountant to determine how you should handle employee taxes.

Basic taxes or simple self-employment forms are easy to prepare, and most people file a 1040 form or the 1040EZ form. Tax forms are available at your local library or online, and they come with thorough instruction books to walk you through each step. You can also use a software program such as TurboTax® or ask your parents to help you fill out the forms. If you have kept good records, this job is doable by anyone — and it is even easier if you have used a software program to categorize and manage your books.

If you have a lot of business expenses, a large amount of revenue, or other extenuating circumstances, it's probably best to hire a certified public accountant (CPA) to prepare your taxes. These folks are on top of the ever-changing tax laws and know how to find the most deductions. More advanced tax issues such as capital gains tax from stock sales or profit-and-loss business statements require expertise that only CPAs can offer. Typically, you can get your taxes prepared for less than $100, so it's worth the money to get it done right and avoid the headache of wading through government forms. Make sure to schedule your appointment early, as accountants get booked up as the April 15 filing deadline approaches. Organize your records well, and go to the meeting with everything in order, especially if your CPA charges by the hour.

Sales tax

As mentioned at the end of Chapter 7, sales tax is a consumption-based tax charged by cities, counties, states, or all three. This tax is a percentage of the product or service price. The customer pays it, and the seller collects it. The seller then sends the sales tax to the appropriate government collection agency. The requirements and amounts for sales tax vary. Some places exempt food or clothing from sales tax, while others charge sales tax for prepared meals or "luxury" foods such as soda.

Check with your state's revenue office for details on the necessary sales tax collection as it relates to your product or service. Visit the website **www.sba.gov**, and look for the link to your state's revenue office. Be sure to check the rules for every state you do business in, as these laws apply to where the sale is made and not where the seller lives. Sales tax also can apply to Internet sales, and legislation is moving through many state governments to address this issue. As most laws stand now, it's the buyer's responsibility to pay sales tax for purchases made over the Internet.

Liability

When you are in charge of a business, you're also responsible for anything that goes wrong. This means you are "liable" for repairing, replacing, or remedying any situations that occur while you are in charge. Sometimes these situations can be extreme or expensive, such a car accident or a home burglary. You'll also be expected to understand and hold the necessary permits or licenses, such as a food permit for selling food. Additionally, you can be sued for using someone else's name, logo, or business idea without permission, sometimes referred to as "infringement." Conversely, you might develop an idea or business name that needs to be protected from others. All these issues are considered liabilities because they can incur large expenses and even lawsuits if not covered through insurance, licensing, or patents. Seek the help of a professional to make sure you have the necessary coverage. These coverages might involve additional expenses, so be sure to include those in your budgeting.

Insurance

People take out insurance to cover the costs of unexpected and potentially expensive events such as a home fire, a burglary, or a catastrophic illness. Insurance companies write a policy that agrees to provide payment for remedying the situation either through a cash payment or reimbursement and replacement of the loss. You pay a premium for this policy, and the value of the item you are insuring determines the cost of the premium. Many policies come with a "deductible," a set amount you will be required to pay before the insurance coverage kicks in. You can buy an insurance policy for just about anything — big movie stars even insure their hair, legs, or voice. The most common policies applicable to your situation will be:

- Auto insurance. This covers your vehicle, occupants and drivers of the vehicle, and other vehicles or people involved in accidents. Most states require insurance coverage on all vehicles. Some policies include additional elements such as roadside assistance.

- Homeowner's or renter's insurance. These policies cover the home, the contents of the home, personal injury accidents that occur on the property, and losses due to fire, burglary, or natural disasters. Equipment used for business or space used for conducting business usually are excluded from the basic homeowner's policy.

- Business or liability insurance. If you are dealing with people such as children or pets or purchasing expensive equipment that is exempt from homeowner's insurance, you will need a separate business policy. This will cover replacing your equipment or paying for injuries or lawsuits that occur while you are caring for others.

- Warranties. These are not true insurance policies, but they are worth mentioning if you're buying expensive equipment. Most purchases are covered by a replacement or repair warranty — be sure to review the terms of the warranty, register your purchase, and file the documents for easy access if something breaks down. By registering your purchase, you'll also be notified if the item is recalled or needs safety upgrades.

Policy coverage and restrictions vary widely by insurance company, your personal situation, and the requirements of your city or state. Review the exemptions and exclusions carefully before purchasing a policy, as some have a waiting period before the policy takes effect. In most situations, your parents' current policy should cover you. Check with your parents and their insurance agent to confirm any coverage issues. If you do need to buy insurance coverage, shop around for the best deal, and make sure to record this as a business expense, as it will be tax deductible.

Licenses and permits

Each job listing talked about the circumstances in which you might need a license or permit to operate your business. These can include everything from a basic driver's license to a tour guide operator's permit. As a small, one-person operation, licensing and permits are not critical to your business unless you are selling food or operating in an industry with health and safety risks. However, if you decide to make your business more official, you'll need a federal, state, or local license to operate. The type of license you need depends on where you live and the type of business you are doing.

Driver's license

If you're operating a passenger vehicle, you will need a valid driver's license. Some states put restrictions on young drivers, such as allowing only one passenger for the first six months or no driving after a certain time. Make sure you understand the requirements and restrictions related to your driving situation. If you will be operating large equipment such as a tractor or commercial vehicle, you probably will need an advanced license. Check with your local Department of Motor Vehicles to learn more.

Food, health, or safety permit

If you're working in a field that affects public safety such as preparing food, you will need special training, a permit, a license, or all three. Without these permits in place, you can be fined or shut down. Check with your local extension office or your state's Department of Health for more information. Most of these licenses require special training, so give yourself a few months to acquire the permit.

Industry-specific licenses and permits

Many cities, counties, and states set their own limits on the types of businesses that need licenses to operate. These often are focused on businesses that affect others, such as day cares; those that could harm the environment, such as mining or farming; and those that could be disruptive to other businesses, such as musicians or tour guides. Inquire at your city hall or ask others in your field of work.

TIP!

Most licenses are not transferable if the business changes ownership, and only those with proper training can operate under the permit.

The SBA website offers an easy search tool to determine if you need a license for your business. You can search by your zip code, your state, and your industry. You'll also find everything you need to know about applying for and working under licensure. Visit the link at: **www.sba.gov/content/business-licenses-and-permits**.

Acquiring and maintaining your license

The department issuing your license will provide the specifics needed to acquire it — you'll need to submit an application with information about your business and proof of your qualifications. You'll be charged for this license, so bring your checkbook. This fee is tax deductible, so be sure to record it in your accounting log.

After you receive your license or permit, read the requirements, and take special care to follow all the steps listed or your license can become invalid. Considerations include:

- Renewal dates. You'll be required to renew your license on a regular basis. Be sure to record this date on your calendar, and make sure to submit your renewal forms a few months in advance.

- Before sending off your applications, copy all forms and supporting documents, and file these with your business records. Also, keep a copy of the approved license or permit in your files.

- Understand and follow the rules for displaying your license. Most states and localities require a prominent display where customers can see the permit.

- If you change or expand your business, your current license might not apply. Check with your licensing entity to be sure you are covered.

Protecting Your Idea and Avoiding Infringement

Have you ever noticed symbols such as ®, ©, or ™, or the words "patented" or "patent No. 1234" behind a company's name or product? These symbols indicate that the product, service, logo, or artistic creation is protected under a copyright or trademark or registered officially with the government. Companies who feel they have a special product, service, or intellectual property take this step to protect others from using the name or copying their product. The type of registration differs with each the product or service. For example, works of art or music are copyrighted while working products are patented or trademarked.

The process of acquiring these protections is run through the United States Patent and Trademark Office (USPTO), a division of the Department of Commerce. Start at their website, **www.uspto.gov**, to learn the basics of protecting your product and the procedures required to complete the application. This website has links including small business focused links, ways to research existing patents or copyrights, and much more. It's a great place to start if you're thinking about officially registering your product.

Acquiring a patent or registering a trademark is difficult to accomplish on your own. The forms, fees, and documentation require a long, drawn-out process, and if anything is done improperly, your application will be denied. For this reason, most people hire a patent attorney to guide them through the system. Because of the expense involved, most small businesses do not file for these protections and just hope the good business ethics of others will protect them from infringement or theft. If you feel you have invented something unique — and you can make money from it — then pursuing registration can be worth the expense. Start your research on the USPTO website, and schedule a consultation with a patent attorney or legal aid clinic to explore your options.

TIP!

Intellectual properties, which include literary, music, architecture, art, and other "original works of authorship," are covered automatically under U.S. Copyright law. You don't have to file officially for your copyright, but it is recommended for full protection. Visit the "Copyright Refresher" link on the USPTO website for full details.

As you start your business, you must ensure your business name, product, or idea is not infringing on someone else's existing trademark. This is typically not an issue with mini-businesses, but some companies are protective of their trademarks. If you use part or all of the name, logo, or product and the company's lawyers feel you are infringing on their trademark, you can be hit with a "cease and desist" order, which means you must stop using this name or image in your business. If you don't cease using it, the company can sue you. Be careful if you decide to name your company, and pick something unique to your business. Visit the USPTO website and click on the link for Trademark Electronic Search System (TESS) to conduct a free search of registered trademarks. If you are planning to file for your own trademark or patent, your attorney will conduct a search as part of the application process. Research other businesses in your area because they might have a similar name or logo. Even if it's not trademarked, it's not good business etiquette to copy someone else's name.

Do You Need to Name Your Business?

The main reason for attaching a name or logo to your business is to build brand recognition and create an image. This recognition becomes part of an overall marketing strategy. Brand recognition and image are helpful for every size of business, but the expense to develop this recognition is cost-prohibitive for small businesses. Remember that every dollar you spend cuts into your bottom line, and finding a trademark-free name, developing a logo, and registering your name can be expensive and time-consuming. You need the potential for large profits or a long-term business view to make the expense pay off.

Naming your business, though, does make it look more professional, and it's perfectly OK to give your business a name without protecting it with trademarks. Many small businesses have started out in just this way. Remember, though, that without trademark protection, anyone can steal your name, and you will have few ways to get it back. Later sections in this chapter will discuss choosing a formal structure for your business, part of which will be selecting a name for your business.

Tips for choosing a business name

Keep it simple — this is the key to choosing a good business name. Your name must tell your customers who you are and what you do. Your name needs to convey that you are professional and can be trusted to do the job well. Think about how you will use your name. Are you going to make T-shirts or hats? Then you will want a short name that will fit this space. Are you providing a specific service such as cleaning or lawn care? Then include that in your name, such as "Lee's Lawns" or "Jane's Kid Care." If possible, pick something catchy that is easy-to-say and remember, and nothing offensive or cutesy. Avoid using made-up words, acronyms, or a phrase common to your area such as the team mascot's name. For example, if your school mascot is a Viking, your name will get lost in a sea of Vikings. Check your local competition, too, so you do not choose a name similar to someone else in the marketplace, which will confuse your customers or cause them to pick your competition accidentally. Once you have chosen a name, don't alter or change it, or you will lose your brand recognition.

Writing a Business Plan

When you first decided to go out on your own, you had a plan in your head and maybe even something written down on paper. If you used this plan to find work or analyze your business, then you've already developed your first business plan. Anything that guided you or helped you make decisions counts as a plan. Of course, as your business grows, you need something a little more official. If you're looking for partners or investors, you will need a formal business plan for presentations. A business plan can include anything you think is important to your business, including references, projections, and great ideas you have for the future. *See Appendix A for a business plan outline recommended by the U.S. Small Business Administration.* Most business plans require documentation and descriptions relating to these areas:

- An executive summary highlighting your experience and the business' history
- A description of the business, product, or service
- A marketing plan
- A business management plan
- Financial projections and past financial records
- Supporting documentation

Writing a business plan helps you flesh out what you want to accomplish with your business and identify any issues you will face for expansion. It will help you point out potential problems and discover opportunities for making more money. Your business plan will also help you develop and express your personal business philosophy and long-term goals. This will be your road map to the future, and it will change with time, so expect to make alterations as you go along. Visit the SBA website for more information or check the Score website at **www.score.org** and click on the "Templates and Tools" link. This link will take you to a thorough explanation of each element of a proper business plan and walk you through putting your own plan together.

Structuring Your Business

The next step is to develop a real business structure. Up until now, you have been operating as a "sole proprietorship." You are the owner and only employee, and any taxes or liability protections are grouped with your personal life. For instance, you file one income tax form, and any liability coverage you have is covered under a personal insurance policy, such as homeowner's insurance.

It doesn't take a formal legal document to be a sole proprietor — it's the de facto structure for most independent contractors or self-employed workers. This type of operating system works for many people and needs no adjustments. You easily can work as an independent contractor for the rest of your career. However, without a formal business structure in place, you are personally liable for anything that goes wrong because of your business. If your product or service is faulty, if your service causes injury, or if your bills go unpaid, you can be sued for damages. If your business doesn't have enough money or assets to satisfy the lawsuit, you can be forced to use your personal money or assets to pay the bill. As mentioned earlier, proper insurance policies will cover you in many of these instances, but establishing a full separation between you and your business is the only way to protect yourself completely.

This separation comes in the form of incorporating your business or forming a legally recognized business. Once this structure is in place, all monies will go through the corporation, and the business will issue you a paycheck. As with other topics discussed in this chapter, incorporating costs money, is complex, and requires assistance from an attorney. The costs are worthwhile, as you not only will protect your personal assets but also gain some tax advantages and make it easier to transfer ownership later on. The kind of business structure you select depends on what type of business you are in, the level of liability you might face, and your long-term goals for the company. The most common structures include:

Partnership

A partnership is formed when two or more persons join together to run a business. Each person contributes money, property, labor, or skill and expects to share in the profits and losses of the business. A partnership must file an annual information return to report the income, deductions, gains, losses, etc., from its operations, but it does not pay income tax. Instead, it "passes through" any profits or losses to its partners. Each partner includes his or her share of the partnership's income or loss on his or her tax return. When forming a partnership it is recommended to draw up a legal document clearly spelling out each partner's responsibilities, contributions, and share of profits.

Corporation

A corporation is a collection of prospective shareholders who exchange money, property, or both, for the corporation's capital stock. A corporation takes the same deductions as a sole proprietorship to figure its taxable income. A corporation conducts business, realizes net income or loss, pays taxes, and distributes profits to shareholders. In general, an elected board of directors runs each corporation — for this reason owners must give up some control of the management of their business.

Subchapter S Corporation

Subchapter S corporations (or S corporations) are corporations that elect to pass corporate income, losses, deductions, and credit through to their shareholders for federal tax purposes. This type of corporation is limited to having no more than 100 shareholders and allows shareholders to avoid double taxation on the corporate income. Subchapter S corporations do have restrictions including: domestic-only memberships, may not include other partnerships, and have only one class of stock. Small companies frequently choose this type of incorporation because of the tax advantages.

Limited Liability Company (LLC)

This is the most flexible and popular business structure for a small business. Similar to a corporation, owners have limited personal liability for the debts and actions of the LLC. Other features of LLCs are similar to a partnership, including management flexibility and the benefit of pass-through taxation. Ownership can be one person, an unlimited number of people, other corporations, or foreign entities. Both federal and state agencies set requirements for accepted LLCs so be sure to check if your business is allowed. An LLC business entity must file a corporation, partnership, or sole proprietorship tax return.

There are many more details, restrictions, and qualifications with each of these mentioned business structures. Visit the SBA website for more details or find a book at your local library to learn more. Make sure the research you do on these forms is current as laws change frequently regarding issues related to corporations and partnerships.

Taking on a Partner

Partnering with someone can offer both advantages and disadvantages, and you must weigh these carefully before you enter into a legally binding partnership with someone. The advantages include gaining another person to share the workload and expenses, adding someone with more experience or complementary skills, an expanded network of potential customers, and someone to share the stress of running a business. The biggest disadvantages of taking on a partner are giving up control of your company and dividing the profits. With a partner, you will have to make compromises and joint decisions. Be careful of giving up too much control, and make sure your partnership is clearly spelled out in a legal document, such as a partnership agreement described in the previous section.

You must get along well with the person or people you choose as a partner. You don't, however, have to be best buddies and hang out on the weekends. Many business partners rarely socialize outside of the office setting. As long as you can communicate effectively, find solutions to disagreements, and work together toward building the business, your partnership will do well.

As a teen, you might be tempted to go into business with your friends, and this can work out some of the time. With this arrangement, though, the old adage of "never mix friends and money" holds true. You might love to hang out with the person, but day-after-day might drive you crazy eventually. Your friend might be great with people but awful at handling money. If things go wrong with the business relationship, you also could lose this person as a friend. Choose someone with your same outlook toward the business, but also look for a partner who can add a skill or attribute you do not have. Your partner doesn't have to live in the same town as you, either — teaming up with someone in another market can help you expand your sales area into an additional market.

CHAPTER ELEVEN

Your Business Future

You have the plan, the name, the structure, and ideally, the customer base. After some time and a little profit, you might start to see a long-term future for your business. Maybe you'd like to improve things, or you'd like to adjust your business so you can take it with you to college. Maybe you enjoy what you are doing and want to see how far you can take it. People just like you started many of today's biggest businesses. If you're willing to focus on your business and get serious about what you are doing, you could be the next big thing on the market.

By now, you know your business well, and if you've kept good records, you can look through them and find opportunities for improvement. Ramping up your profits and growing your business could be as simple as expanding your product line or bringing on a few employees. This chapter will help you identify areas for growth, find ways to improve your business, and offer ideas for cultivating your existing customer base. It also will walk you through the process of shutting things down if that seems to be the right move for you.

Turning Your Job into a Business

If you have sufficient opportunity for growth and a potential for increased sales, you have the seeds for a successful business. Your first step is to repeat the steps you took to start your business. You'll need to compare your business with the competition, including their prices. Will your expanded business find room in this marketplace, or is it too crowded? Is there a missed opportunity you could capitalize on, and how can you do that?

You have a wonderful market research tool available to you, and that is surveying your existing customer base. Start with informal surveys of your customers or your social network by asking a few questions such as:

- What do you like or dislike about our product or service?
- How often do you use our product or service? What would cause you to use it more often?
- What do you think about our prices?
- Do you buy this elsewhere? If so, why?
- Would you buy X if I added it to the product line? This can include new products or expansions of existing products such as a new color or flavor.

Make sure to reward the customers who take time to answer these questions. Add these answers to your competitive analysis, and you will have a good indication of whether to grow your business. If you think it is worthwhile, it's time to conduct a formal market study such as those offered by market researchers or marketing firms. This will cost you money but is worth the investment. Look in your local yellow pages for firms specializing in this type of research.

Doing a better job

Sometimes increasing your bottom line can be accomplished by improving your current business practices. Take a good, hard look at how you are running your operation. Are things falling through the cracks, or are you overwhelmed? Sometimes changing the little things will increase your profit margin:

- Are you managing your time well? Do you work while you are at work or spend the hours socializing? If so, you're reducing your overall hourly wage.

- Are your appointments and records well organized? Do you spend extra time searching for receipts? Do you forget appointments or show up late to work because you do not keep a good calendar? If so, you might be losing customers.

- Have you had customer complaints or lost customers? What are the reasons for these complaints, and are they ongoing or a one-time occurrence? If so, you might be able to regain these lost customers.

- What are your supplier or vendor relationships like? Do you continue to order from the same company? If so, you might be spending more on overhead than necessary.

- Where and how are you selling your product or finding new customers? Do you keep going back to the same markets but see stagnate or decreasing sales? If so, you might need to expand your selling area.

- Do you feel like you spend a lot of time on non-billable activities, such as paperwork? Do you have more work than you can handle adequately? If so, you might need an assistant, an extra employee, or help from a professional such as an accountant.

Think about how your business is working — or not working — and address the areas you think need fixing. Pick the easiest problem first, find the cheapest solution, and then work your way down this list.

CASE STUDY: ON THE JOB WITH DANIEL NOVAES

Occupation: Founder, Elekteks
Inc, College Media Group LLC
Age: Started his business at age 16
Novaesd182@gmail.com
www.Elekteks.com

Daniel Novaes. Photo
courtesy of Daniel Novaes.

Like most teens, my first job was at a retail store working for minimum wage. It took me all of two weeks to realize this low-paying job was not going to be enough money for me. Fate intervened, and during a trip to a bookstore, I stumbled upon a book about selling things online. I finished that book in two days and knew how I was going to make my money. Problem was, I needed to find something that would sell. After a few failed attempts, I realized I had a great tool right in my neighborhood — an outlet mall where I could pick up discounted items and re-sell them online. In less than twelve hours, I had sold about $600 in leather coats at a total profit of nearly $200. I continued selling these types of items until a stroke of networking luck stepped in to help me.

One of my online customers also sold electronics online. He was highly rated, so I contacted him to see if he sold wholesale items. After the initial "How old are you?" discussion, we talked for nearly an hour. This man, Mr. Juan Mattos, became my mentor and a critical supplier for my new electronics-selling business, Elekteks. Mr. Mattos helped me in numerous ways including extending lines of credit, working with me to drop ship orders, and helping me navigate the world of business. I don't know why he helped me, but I suspect it was because he wanted to give an ambitious teenager a chance to succeed. All it took to find this man and shape my business was one phone call. That is definitely the true spirit of developing your network.

As my business grew, I once again connected with a customer who eventually helped me expand my company even more. He had extensive knowledge and business relationships in the European Union, and with his help, I expanded my business into the international marketplace. Once again, a customer became an important business contact, and it was only because I took the time to nurture that relationship. These were truly the beginnings of my company, and I was still in high school and going off to college. Without these turns of events and my fearless networking approach, I don't know what would have become of my business. I do know that those connections helped me build my business into a multimillion dollar company that is still growing!

Words of Wisdom: Give it a shot and if you fail, then congratulations, you are on your way to becoming a real entrepreneur. As Henry Ford once said, "Failure is only the opportunity to begin again, only this time more wisely."

Advancing your skills

Another way to up your bottom line is educate yourself in advanced areas as they relate to your business. For example, if you're currently offering lawn mowing and raking, learn how to prune bushes or trim trees, and offer this as an additional service. Advancing your skills means pushing yourself to get better at the job you are currently doing. After you have been doing these tasks for awhile, you should be faster at finishing and putting out a higher quality product than when you started.

TIP!

Never underestimate the value of efficiency. Remember the faster you work, the more you will make per hour, but keep in mind that too fast might lead to poor quality.

If you can offer more services or add value to your current products, you can expand your sales without adding new customers. If your existing or former customers are satisfied, they will be happy to look over the extras you offer. It can be as simple as saying "Hey, did you know I have added three new colors to my line of T-shirts?" Make sure you aren't pushy when selling them extra — just letting them know you have added a service is enough to get the ball rolling.

Using mentors or joining trade groups

A great way to improve your skills and connect with others is to join a trade group or seek a mentor. In many cases, your customers can be mentors, if they're willing to help you learn. For example, if you've been hired to help someone work on their home, ask them to teach you a carpentry skill. You won't be paid for this time, but most adults love to help teens who are interested in learning. Go online or check your local newspaper for trade groups or business-oriented seminars scheduled in your area. You also can find great mentorship connections at the SBA website.

Continuing customer service

Increasing sales doesn't mean continuously seeking out new customers. Sometimes it can be as easy as nurturing the group of customers you already have. All the lessons talked about in Chapter 8 under "Finding new customers" apply when keeping your current customers happy. A happy customer will buy more and recommend you to their friends — and you don't have to spend any extra time or effort reaching this customer. Keep an eye on customer comments, and make sure you're doing all you can to keep them happy, including:

- Fixing problems quickly and with a smile
- Thanking them for their business
- Rewarding faithful customers with added bonuses
- Helping them identify additional needs you can satisfy
- Asking them for referrals respectfully

How to Take Your Job with You to College

Moving away to college doesn't mean shuttering your business. In fact, self-employed work fits with a hectic college schedule and probably will earn you more than jobs you will find on campus. The easiest jobs to take along with you are service-related jobs such as cleaning, cooking, dog walking, and personal care. No matter where you live, people need these jobs done. However, if you're looking for work in a college town, a wide pool of students probably is competing for these same jobs. If your job involves producing or selling products, it might be more challenging to transfer these jobs to a dorm room. It can be done, but you will need to plan ahead and have an understanding roommate.

Taking your job with you involves all the steps you needed to go through when beginning your business. You'll need to assess your new market for competition, customer need, and availability. You'll have to reconsider the logistical aspects of operating in a new location, especially transportation if you are not bringing a car with you. Make sure any insurance policies you depend on will include coverage if you are in a different area. Finally, what will you do with the customers you have at home? If you're planning to come back for summer breaks, maybe you can find a way to resume working for these clients when you return.

Shutting Your Business Down

The time might come when you need to make the tough decision of shutting your business down. Situations in your life might be changing, and ending your business is not necessarily considered a failure. There are many good reasons to stop doing business, including:

1. You're not making enough money or lack the potential to make an adequate income.

2. You have reached your goals.

3. Work is negatively impacting other areas of your life, especially your grades.

4. You're moving to college.

5. You don't like what you're doing.

6. You feel unsafe or uncomfortable at your work.

Talk with your parents or another trusted adult, and ask their opinion on what to do. If you decide it is time to be done, end your business in a professional manner, and be sure to honor all the commitments you have made in promised products, payments, or appointments. If you must cancel or cannot fulfill your obligations, give your customers lots of advance notice or offer to help them find a replacement. By ending your relationship in this way, you will keep the door open if you decide to reopen your business. Follow up your closure with a heartfelt thank you to all your good customers, and remember to ask for references whenever possible. Remember to delete or change any website links, phone numbers, or advertising pieces currently running in the market. Hang on to all your records, so you can file your income taxes for the year.

Can you hand off your business?

If you are closing your business because you are moving away or are too busy, consider handing off your valued customers to a friend or younger sibling. Just make sure they are able to maintain your level of service, and be sure to inform your customers of the changeover. At this point, it is best to completely hand over everything and remove your name from the business. If you have equipment, product inventory, or any other valuable business assets, you can expect to charge the new owners for these items. You won't be paid full price for used equipment but new, unopened materials or products can be sold at the price you paid for them. A simple hand-off such as this is only possible for a sole proprietorship. If your business is incorporated or in a partnership arrangement, you will need to work with a lawyer to shut it down or sell it off.

Selling off Your Business

This is the final stop and the ultimate success every startup business hopes for. Sure, you love what you do, you are probably making good money, and you might have big plans for the future — but if the right offer comes along, anything is for sale. This offer might come in the form of a franchising agreement or licensing arrangement with which you can retain some ownership. Most franchising agreements include granting another company or person exclusive rights to your product, name, idea, or logo. In exchange for these rights, you will be paid a one-time fee or a royalty of all future sales.

As with selling shares or incorporating, you will have to give up a lot of control when you enter into such an agreement. The person you have sold rights to might use your product in a manner that you do not agree with. Franchising and licensing agreements take many forms, and you can negotiate almost anything into your contract. For this reason, work with a business attorney experienced in this area to craft the best deal. Never agree to an offer to "buy your product" or "franchise your idea" until you have a qualified business attorney examine every document.

You Can Do It!

When you started this book, you were probably curious and cautiously optimistic about going out on your own to make money. After all, people before you have made millions. Why shouldn't you? Ideally, this book has turned your spark of an idea into fireworks and armed you with the knowledge and confidence you need to get out there and start your big adventure.

If you skimmed through the case studies of successful teens, you probably noticed a theme. Without fail, every teen said, "I love what I do, I make more money than my peers, and the good parts greatly outweigh the bad."

These teens were all just like you when they started their businesses. They were looking for an alternative to traditional teen jobs, and they wanted to shape their own career paths from the beginning. They were also able to build their financial future and learn valuable lessons they could take with them into adulthood. In nearly every situation, these teens ran into obstacles, but they weren't deterred from their goals. With good mentors, a positive attitude, and a willingness to learn from mistakes, they succeeded and achieved their life dreams.

With what you have learned here, you, too, can take your passions, refine them into a doable idea, and get into making money. You might not come out of your work experience a millionaire, but you will gain a treasure trove of experience because you have taken on this challenge. As you will hear in any high school commencement speech, "This is not the end, but the beginning of your future." Cliché, yes, but true here, too. You have made it to the end of this book, but you are just starting down your path of working. Whether you like it or not, this path is going to weave through your entire life, and you have at least 50 years of work ahead of you. One lesson we hope you've taken from this book is that work doesn't have to be a dirty four-letter word. You can enjoy what you do, you can shape your future, and if you love what you do, it will not seem like work at all.

Good luck, and we can't wait to see what you'll accomplish.

Sample Business Documents

Example of a Business Card

Dave's Handyman Service

Help around the house, yard, garage, or just about anywhere

597-555-1234

Example of a Poster, Flier, or Small Display Ad

Dave's Handyman Service

Is your to-do list longer than ever? Would you like to start crossing things off that list and have more time for fun? Call in Dave and he'll get it done!

Dave can do just about anything!

- ✓ In-home fix it jobs
- ✓ Regular home maintenance work
- ✓ Garage, basement, or attic cleaning and organizing
- ✓ Yard projects
- ✓ Simple construction or repair
- ✓ Furniture assembly
- ✓ Anything that needs muscle

597-555-1234

Call today! Free estimates and fast service!

Example of a Cold Call Script

The situation: You want to find five lawns to mow this summer. Your neighbor, Tom Jones, has already hired you, and you politely ask him if he knows of anyone else looking for yard help. He gives you the name and phone number of his golf buddy, Joe Brown. This is the script of your cold call:

Mr. Brown: Hello?

You: Hi, Mr. Brown, my name is John Smith. Your friend, Tom Jones, said I should call you.

Mr. Brown: OK, what can I do for you?

You: Well, I'm a sophomore up at Franklin High School, and I'm trying to find some lawn mowing jobs during summer break. I live next door to Mr. Jones, and he hired me to mow his lawn this summer. He thought you might be in need of help, too.

At this point, Mr. Brown will either say no or ask a few questions regarding your prices, your services, and so on. If he says no, politely thank him for his time and hang up. If he seems interested, you can offer to stop by his house and discuss your business in more detail or offer to do the job once for a reduced rate before he commits to hiring you long term. Negotiating skills will come in at this point, and as long as you are confident and know your business well, you will do just fine.

Example of a Teen Résumé

Dave Smith

7982 Maine Street, Any Town, Any State, 12345 (555)123-4567, dave@email.com

SKILLS

Work well with people

Good at problem solving

Experienced in carpentry, lawn care, and general handyman works

Proficient in basic computer skills including MSWord, Excel, and PowerPoint

WORK EXPERIENCE

Johnson's Hardware Store, Summer 2011

Job duties included: customer service, unloading delivery trucks, stocking shelves, home deliveries, and general knowledge of hardware store supplies.

Volunteer Home Helper, St. Martin's Youth Group, 2009 to Present

Assist with various home repair and fix-it needs for members of our community.

ACTIVITIES

Football, Wrestling, and Baseball Varsity, 2009 to Present

First Chair, Trumpet, High School Band, 2008 to Present

High School Debate Club, 2010 to Present

Math League, 2008 to Present

EDUCATION

My Town High School, Expected graduation June 2013, GPA 3.5

REFERENCES

My Coach – 555-1234, coach@coach.com

My Teacher – 555-6789, teacher@teacher.com

My trusted neighbor – 555-1011, neighbor@neighbor.com

Business Plan Outline

This outline is available at **www.sba.gov/content/templates-writing-business-plan** *with full explanations of each item.*

Elements of a business plan

1. Cover sheet
2. Executive summary (statement of the business purpose)
3. Table of contents
4. Body of the document
   A. Business
      1. Description of business
      2. Marketing
      3. Competition
      4. Operating procedures
      5. Personnel
      6. Business insurance
   B. Financial data
      1. Loan applications
      2. Capital equipment and supply list
      3. Balance sheet
      4. Break-even analysis
      5. Profit and loss statements
      6. Three-year summary
      7. Detail by month, first year
      8. Detail by quarters, second and third year
      9. Assumptions upon which projections were based
      10. Pro forma cash flow

    C. Supporting documents

        1. Tax returns of principals (partners in the business) for last three years, personal financial statements (all banks have these forms)

        2. Copy of franchise contract and all supporting documents provided by the franchisor (for franchise businesses)

        3. Copy of proposed lease or purchase agreement for building space

        4. Copy of licenses and other legal documents

        5. Copy of resumes of all principals

        6. Copies of letters of intent from suppliers, etc.

Freelance Contract Elements

This is an example is taken from the SBA website and includes descriptions of common topics you can use to draft a contract template for your business:

Contact Information

- Include the name and business address, phone, email address, and any other relevant contact information for you and your client.

Project Description

- Detail the job or project description including specific information on what the client is getting — and what the client is not getting — as a result of this contract. Thoroughly document the agreement to prevent any confusion on either end.

Milestone Dates

- Document the contract dates of service from start date to end date.

- Document all milestone dates, including when drafts, phases, and completed works will be completed.

Rates and Fees

- Record your rate structure for the project (hourly rate or a flat rate.) If you are charging an hourly rate, estimate the expected number of hours per project phase, and include it in this section. Will your client cover the cost of materials, or is that worked into your fee? Clarify how these expenses are covered.

- Include a description of your invoicing procedures, including when you expect payment (weekly, monthly, etc.) and if or how penalties apply if your client delivers payment late or not at all.

Ownership, Cancellation, and Redos

- Your contract should explicitly say who owns what rights (copyrights, patents, etc.) to the finished work.

- Be sure to include a cancellation clause in your contract that explains the procedure if your client cancels the project. This should include your compensation and ownership rights for any unfinished work.

- What if your client is unsatisfied with your work, or wants you to redo a portion of it? Include a section in your contract on your revision policy.

Signatures

- When you and your client are satisfied with the terms of the contract, both parties must sign the contract to make it legally binding.

Example of an Invoice

Dave's Handyman Service   INVOICE #0001

7982 Maine Street, Any Town, Any State, 12345   TO: _____
(555)123-4567, dave@email.com   _____
                                                          _____

DATE	DESCRIPTION	AMOUNT
	TOTAL	

Helpful Resources – Websites and Books

Online Sites for Finding Work or Selling Your Products

Websites abound to find work in every area of business. These websites, however, are constantly changing, growing, and expanding. The websites listed here are current as of the writing of this book. When looking for online jobs, do a quick search under "independent contractor" or "freelancer," plus the field you are interested in. Use only sites with secure systems, preferably beginning with https. Research the site thoroughly, look for independent reviews, and check the feedback of anyone you are working with. Read any registration files before you agree to pay for membership or registration fees. In many cases, these fees are minimal and worth the price, while other sites charge exorbitant fees for little return. Look for a secure payment or escrow system that allows you to pay with a credit card or bank account in which your account information or card numbers are hidden from the other party.

These listings show the area of work, followed by a suggested website:

Artwork: **www.thejulygroup.com**, **www.artfire.com** (fine art), **www.guru.com**, **www.elance.com**, **www.freelancer.com** (graphic design and commercial artwork)

Antiques, vintage, and collectibles: **www.etsy.com**, **www.ebay.com**, **www.craigslist.org**

Beta, software, or video game testing: **www.elance.com**, **www.guru.com**

Computer programming and software development: **www.sologig.com**, **www.elance.com**

Crafts and handmade products: **www.etsy.com**, **www.ebay.com**, **www.artfire.com**, **www.zibbet.com**

Data entry and word processing: **www.simplyhired.com**, **www.elance.com**, **www.sologig.com**

Editing: **www.elance.com**, **www.sologig.com**, **www.guru.com**

Foreign language translation or transcription: **www.elance.com**, **www.simplyhired.com**, **www.sologig.com**

Online surveys: **www.bigspot.com**, **www.mindfieldonline.com**, **www.myhotspex.com** (Be wary of online survey sites, as many are scams.)

Photography: **www.guru.com**, **www.elance.com**, **www.simplyhired.com** (commercial uses), **www.artfire.com**, **www.etsy.com**, **www.zibbet.com** (art photography)

Song writing: **www.guru.com**, **www.elance.com**, **www.freelancer.com** (commercial use such as jingles), **www.songwritingopportunities.com** (lyrics and musical scores)

Transcription services: **www.simplyhired.com**, **www.elance.com**, **www.sologig.com**

Writing: **www.guru.com**, **www.elance.com**, **www.freelancer.com** (marketing, advertising, non-fiction, public relations), **www.writersdigest.com** (writing contests and listing of magazine markets)

Online Business Resources

As mentioned in the previous section, websites change and evolve constantly, so be sure to search for information specific to your field. The most reputable sites will end with .gov or .edu. Sites ending in .org, .net, or .com can provide a lot of good information but will include marketing and potentially dangerous links to other sites.

326   The Teen's Ultimate Guide to Making Money When You Can't Get a Job

Websites

No. 1 Best Site to Start With: **www.sba.gov** (site for the Small Business Administration with everything you need to know or links to find it elsewhere.)

Accounting and finances: **www.score.org**, **www.accountingcoach.com**

Babysitter and CPR training: **www.redcross.org**

Banking and money: **www.fdic.gov** (banking protections), **www.econedlink.org** (savings calculator), **www.fool.com/teens/teens03.htm** (investing)

Cleaning and household tips: **www.heloise.com**

Consumer awareness and Internet safety: **www.lookstogoodtobetrue.com** (click the "Teen Center" link)

Consumer protection: **www.bbb.org**

Cost estimating calculator and bid assistance: **www.costhelper.com**

Credit cards: **www.federalreserve.gov/consumerinfo**, **www.bankrate.com**

Department of Labor: **www.dol.gov** (click the Youth & Labor link)

Food safety: **www.foodsafety.gov**

Franchising your business: **www.franchise.org**

General business information and teen mentoring network:
www.ceospaceinternational.com, **www.ja.org**, **www.score.org**

Grants: **www.grants.gov**

Health and safety work rules for teens: **www.youthrules.dol.gov**,
www.cusucceed.net

Interest inventory: **www.learnmoreindiana.org** (look for
"career clickers")

Investing: **www.fool.com**

Junior Achievement site: **www.ja.org**

Licensing and permits:
www.sba.gov/content/business-licenses-and-permits

Patents, trademarks, copyrights: **www.uspto.gov**

Survey creation: **www.zoomerang.com**

Taxes: **www.sba.gov** (look for the link to your state's revenue office),
www.irs.gov, **www.bankrate.com**

Books

101 Businesses You Can Start For Less Than One Thousand Dollars: For Students, by Heather L. Shepard, published by Atlantic Publishing, 2007

A Complete Guide to Personal Finance: For Teenagers and College Students, by Tamsen Butler, published by Atlantic Publishing, 2010

Babysitting Jobs: The Business of Babysitting, by Barbara Mehlman, published by Capstone Press, 2007

Life Lists for Teens: Tips, Steps, Hints, and How-Tos for Growing Up, Getting Along, Learning, and Having Fun, by Pamela Espeland, published by Free Spirit Publishing, 2003

Start it Up, by Kenrya Rankin, published by Orange Avenue Publishing, 2011

The Big Enough Company, by Adelaide Lancaster and Amy Abrams, published by Penguin Group, 2011

The Element: How Finding Your Passion Changes Everything, by Ken Robinson, published by Penguin Group, 2009

The Motley Fool Investment Guide for Teens, by David and Tom Gardner, published by Simon and Schuster, 2002

What Color Is Your Parachute? For Teens, 2nd Edition: Discovering Yourself, Defining Your Future, by Carol Christen and Richard N. Bolles, published by Ten Speed Press, 2010

Bibliography

Averkamp, Harold. *What Are Sales Tax?* 2011.
  www.blog.accountingcoach.com

Bielagus, Peter G. *Quick Cash for Teens*. Sterling Publishing Co., 2009.

Butler, Tamsen. *A Complete Guide to Personal Finance: For Teenagers and College Students*. Atlantic Publishing, 2010.

Christen, Carol and Bolles, Richard N. *What Color is Your Parachute?* Ten Speed Press, 2010.

CU Succeed. *Summer Job Pitfalls & Good Ideas*. 2011.
  www.cusucceed.net

Gardner, David and Gardner, Tom. *Motley Fool Investment Guide for Teens*. Simon and Schuster, 2002.

Gengler, Colleen. *Survival Guide for Parents of Teenagers: I Need to Get A Job*. Adapted and revised from: *Positive Parenting of Teens, Teens and Employment*. 2011. **www.extension.umn.edu**

Harmon, Daniel E. *First Job Smarts*. The Rosen Publishing Group, 2010

Ireland, Susan. *The Complete Idiot's Guide to Cool Jobs for Teens*. Pearson Education, 2001.

Lancaster, Adelaide and Abrams, Amy. *The Big Enough Company*. Penguin Group, 2011.

Maranjian, Selena. *What to Expect From Investing*. 2011. **www.fool.com**

Mariotti, Steve. *The Young Entrepreneur's Guide to Starting and Running a Business*. Three Rivers Press, 2000.

Mehlman, Barbara. *Babysitting Jobs*. Capstone Press, 2007

Rankin, Kenrya. *Start It Up*. San Francisco, California: Orange Avenue Publishing, 2011.

Riehm, Sarah L. *50 Great Businesses for Teens*. Surrey Books, 1997.

Roza, Greg. *Great Networking Skills*. The Rosen Publishing Group, 2008.

Shepard, Heather L. *101 Businesses You Can Start for Less Than One Thousand Dollars: For Students*. Atlantic Publishing, 2007.

Topp, Carol. *Starting a Micro Business*. Ambassador Publishing, 2010.

About the Author

Julie Fryer lives with her husband, two sons, and vizsla dog in southeastern Minnesota. Julie is a freelance writer who writes nonfiction articles and books focusing on self-help, organic and green living, and everyday living. She is the author of *The Complete Guide to Your New Root Cellar* and *The Complete Guide to Water Storage*, and a contributing writer to various magazines and online websites including **myorganicgardeningblog.com**.

When she is not writing, Julie and her family love to fish in area trout streams, enjoy summer camping and boat trips, and tend a large vegetable and flower garden.

Index